Essential
Swedish Grammar

JULIAN GRANBERRY

Director, Multicultural Associates
Horseshoe Beach, Florida

Dover Publications, Inc., New York

Copyright © 1991 by Dover Publications, Inc.
All rights reserved under Pan American and International Copyright Conventions.

Published in Canada by General Publishing Company, Ltd., 30 Lesmill Road, Don Mills, Toronto, Ontario.
Published in the United Kingdom by Constable and Company, Ltd., 3 The Lanchesters, 162–164 Fulham Palace Road, London W6 9ER.

Essential Swedish Grammar is a new work, first published by Dover Publications, Inc., in 1991.

Manufactured in the United States of America
Dover Publications, Inc., 31 East 2nd Street, Mineola, N.Y. 11501

Library of Congress Cataloging-in-Publication Data

Granberry, Julian.
    Essential Swedish grammar   /   Julian Granberry.
        p.   cm.
    Includes index.
    ISBN 0-486-26953-1
    1. Swedish language—Grammar—1950–   I. Title.
PD5112.5.G73   1991
439.782'421—dc20
                                                                    91-3707
                                                                    CIP

CONTENTS

INTRODUCTION

Essential Swedish Grammar assumes that you have a limited amount of time at your disposal to study Swedish and that your objective is simple everyday communication, both spoken and written. This book, therefore, does not attempt to offer a complete outline of all aspects of Swedish grammar, even in a highly condensed form. It does, however, offer a series of aids to help you use more effectively phrases and words that you have already learned. This book will introduce you to the most common structures and forms of Swedish and a selected number of the most useful rules.

How to Study *Essential Swedish Grammar*

If you have already studied Swedish in a conventional manner, this book will serve as a review, and you can use it by glancing through all of it quickly and then selecting those areas on which you wish to concentrate.

If, however, this is your first acquaintance with Swedish grammar, the following suggestions may be of help:

1. Before beginning to work your way through this book, master several hundred useful phrases and expressions such as you will find in any good phrase book or in the *Listen & Learn Swedish* course. The material in this book will be much more easily understood after you have achieved some simple working knowledge of the language. This book's purpose is to enable you to gain greater fluency once you have learned phrases and expressions, not to teach you to construct sentences from rules and vocabulary.

2. Read through *Essential Swedish Grammar* at least once in its entirety. Do not be concerned if some of the material is not immediately clear; what appears to be discouragingly complex on first reading will become much simpler as you progress in your study. The first reading is necessary to acquaint you with the terms and concepts used from the beginning. Learning these will help you improve your comprehension of Swedish and use more freely the expressions and words you already know. As you use Swedish and hear it spoken, many of its grammatical patterns will become familiar to you. *Essential Swedish Grammar* helps you discover these patterns, and it will be helpful to you as you develop your vocabulary and improve your comprehension.

3. Go back to this book periodically. Sections that at first seem difficult or of doubtful benefit may prove extremely helpful as you progress further.

4. For the most part, *Essential Swedish Grammar* follows a logical order, taking up the main divisions of grammar in sequence. You will do best to follow this order. However, you may be one of those who learn best when they study to answer an immediate question or need (e.g., how to form the comparative of adjectives; how to conjugate "to be," etc.). If you are such a student, turn to the section that interests you at the moment, but read through the entire section and not just an isolated part. Individual remarks, taken out of context, are easily misunderstood and may seriously mislead you.

5. Examples are given for every rule. It will be helpful if you memorize them. If you learn all the examples in *Essential Swedish Grammar,* you will have encountered the basic difficulties of Swedish and studied models for their solution.

6. You cannot study Swedish or any other language systematically without an understanding of grammar, and the use and understanding of grammatical terms is as essential as a knowledge of certain mechanical terms when you learn to drive a car. If your knowledge of grammatical terms is a little hazy, read the Glossary of Grammatical Terms (p. 70) and refer to it whenever necessary.

In Swedish, as in any language, there are potentially many ways to express a single idea. Some involve simple constructions, others more difficult ones. Some of the more difficult constructions may well be more sophisticated ways of conveying the thought and ones that you will ultimately wish to master, but during your first experiments in communication in Swedish, you can achieve your aim by using a simple construction. Be satisfied at first with the simplest.

You should not, however, be afraid of making mistakes. The purpose of this book is not to teach you to speak like a native but to allow you to communicate and be understood. If you pay attention to what you're doing, you will find that eventually you will make fewer and fewer errors. Sooner or later you'll be able to review *Essential Swedish Grammar* or a more detailed book at a time that is appropriate for polishing your speech.

As you begin to speak Swedish, you will be your own best judge of those areas where you need most help. If there is no one with you, you can practice by speaking mentally to yourself. In the course of the day see how many simple thoughts that you have expressed in English you are able to turn into Swedish. This kind of experimental self-testing will give direction to your study of Swedish. Remember that your purpose in studying this course in Swedish is not to pass an examination or receive a certificate, but to communicate with others on a simple but useful level. *Essential Swedish Grammar* should not be thought of as the equivalent of a formal course of study at a university. Although it could serve as a useful supplement to such a course, its primary aim is to help adults study on their own. Of course, no self-study or academic course, or even series of courses, will ever be ideally suited to all students. You must rely on and be guided by your own rate of learning and your own requirements and interests.

SUGGESTIONS FOR VOCABULARY BUILDING

1. Study words and word lists that answer real and immediate personal needs. If you are planning to travel in the near future, your motivation and orientation are clear-cut, and *Listen & Learn Swedish* or another good travel phrase book will provide you with the material you need. Select material according to your personal interests and requirements. Even if you do not plan to travel to Sweden in the near future, you will probably learn more quickly by imagining yourself in a travel situation.

2. Memorize by association. Phrase books usually give associated word lists. If you use a dictionary, don't memorize words at random but words that are related in some fashion.

3. Study the specialized vocabulary of your profession, business or hobby. If you are interested in real estate, learn the many terms associated with property, buying, selling, leasing, etc. An interest in mathematics could lead you to learn a wide vocabulary in that discipline. You will quickly learn words in your own specialty and a surprising amount will be applicable or transferable to other areas. Although specialized vocabularies may not always be readily available, an active interest and a good dictionary will help you get started.

4. Swedish, like English, contains many compound words, and this will make vocabulary building much simpler than it might otherwise seem. If you can recognize the component parts of a compound, you will be able in many instances to understand the meaning of the new word. The following list gives examples of such compound forms:

SWEDISH	ENGLISH
avtaga	take off, remove [LIT.: off take]
handmålad	hand painted [LIT.: hand painted]
inbjuda	invite [LIT.: in bid]
järnväg	railway [LIT.: iron way]
landsväg	highway [LIT.: land way]

LIST OF ABBREVIATIONS

Abbreviations used in *Essential Swedish Grammar*

ADJ.	Adjective
COM.	Common
CONDIT.	Conditional
DEF.	Definition
INT.	Interrogative
LIT.	Literally
NEUT.	Neuter
PART.	Participle
PERF.	Perfect
PERS.	Person
PL.	Plural
REL.	Relative
SING.	Singular

NOTE: Whenever the Swedish construction is basically different from the construction in English, a *literal* translation enclosed in square brackets is given to help you analyze and understand the Swedish syntax. This literal translation is immediately followed by a translation into idiomatic English.

PRONUNCIATION

The Alphabet

The Swedish alphabet consists of the following twenty-nine letters:

SWEDISH LETTERS	VOWEL LENGTH	PRONUNCIATION
a	(LONG)	as in father
	(SHORT)	like the *u* in much
b		*b*
c		like the *s* in sit when followed by *e*, *i* or *y*; otherwise, like the *k* in sky
d		as in day*
e	(LONG)	like the *a* in face
	(SHORT)	between the *e* in bet and the *a* in hat
	(MUTE)	as in happening
f		*f*
g		like the *y* in yes when followed by *e*, *i*, *y*, *ä* or *ö* in a stressed syllable; otherwise, as in go
h		as in hand
i	(LONG)	as in machine
	(SHORT)	as in bid
j		like the *y* in yes
k		like the *ch* in German *ich* when followed by *e*, *i*, *y*, *ä* or *ö* in a stressed syllable; otherwise, as in sky
l		as in sleep
m		*m*
n		as in night*

---

*This sound is formed with the tip of the tongue against the teeth, not against the back of the gums (alveolar ridge).

SWEDISH LETTERS	VOWEL LENGTH	PRONUNCIATION
o	(LONG)	as in f*oo*d
	(SHORT)	as in g*oo*d
p		*p*
q		like the *k* in s*k*y
r		like the rolled tongue-tip Spanish *r**
s		as in *s*ing
t		as in *t*ouch**
u	(LONG)	a tightly pronounced long *u*-sound peculiar to Swedish
	(SHORT)	between the *oo* in g*oo*d and the *u* in h*u*t
v		*v*
w		*w* or *v*
x		as in rela*x*
y	(LONG)	like the *ü* in German m*ü*de
	(SHORT)	a more clipped pronunciation of the long *y*
z		like the *s* in *s*it
å	(LONG)	like the *o* in h*o*me
	(SHORT)	like the *o* in German h*o*ffen
ä	(LONG)	like the *e* in French m*e*r
	(SHORT)	like the *ai* in French m*ai*son
ö	(LONG)	like the *eu* in French p*eu*
	(SHORT)	a more clipped pronunciation of the long *ö*

NOTE: The letters *b, d, g, j, l, m, n, r* and *v* are voiced consonants; *f, h, k, p, s* and *t* are voiceless consonants. The letters *q* and *w* occur only in a few proper names in Swedish. The letter *z* is found only in a few foreign words.

---

*When *r* precedes the consonants *d, l, n* or *t*, the resulting combination is pronounced as a single consonant: the *r* is not heard, but the other consonant is pronounced with the tip of the tongue against the back of the gums. The combination *rs* is pronounced *sh* as in *sh*ip.

**This sound is formed with the tip of the tongue against the teeth, not against the back of the gums (alveolar ridge).

Spelling

As is the case in English, the correspondence between spelling and pronunciation in Swedish is not exact. The same sounds can be represented by different symbols:

1. dj
g
gj $\left.\right\}$ = *y* in *y*es
hj
j
lj

2. rs
sch
sj $\left.\right\}$ = *sh* in *sh*ip
skj
stj

Stress

In Swedish (as in English), words have strong syllabic stress. In the majority of purely Swedish words, the principal stress falls on the first syllable. The other syllables may have either no stress or secondary stress. Secondary stress in Swedish is, however, often much stronger than in English and can be divided into strong and weak secondary stress.

Principal Stress

Although the principal stress falls generally on the first syllable of a word, there are a few important exceptions to this rule. The principal stress falls: (1) on the second syllable of words beginning with the prefix *be-* or *för-;* (2) on the *-e-* in verbs ending in *-era;* (3) on the last syllable in words of French origin.

Strong Secondary Stress

Strong secondary stress falls: (1) on the second part of a compound word; (2) on suffixes including *-dom, -het, -lek, -skap* and *-sam*.

Weak Secondary Stress

Weak secondary stress or no stress falls on the second syllable of words of two or more syllables that are not compounds.

Long and Short Vowels

One important way in which Swedish vowels differ from English vowels is in sound length. Swedish has nine short vowels and nine long vowels. A long vowel can occur only in a stressed syllable. Vowels are always short in unstressed syllables. In a stressed syllable the vowel is generally long if it is followed by only one consonant or by no consonant at all, and short if followed by more than one consonant:

LONG VOWEL	SHORT VOWEL
tak (roof)	tack (thanks)
mat (food)	mast (mast)

A long vowel in the uninflected form of a word usually remains long in inflected forms. However, the long vowel of a noun is sometimes shortened before the genitive ending -s.

Use of Capital Letters

As in English, the names of countries and places are written with capital letters in Swedish (e.g., *Sverige,* Sweden; *Stockholm*). However, in distinction from English, nouns denoting nationality and languages, or adjectives derived from proper names are written with small letters (e.g., *engelska,* English; *parisiska,* Parisian). Names of days, months, festivals and titles are also written with small letters (e.g., *fredag,* Friday; *augusti,* August; *påsk,* Easter; *professor Svensson*).

Punctuation

In Swedish (unlike English), a comma is used to separate dependent from independent clauses even when the conjunction *att* (that) is used:

Han visste, att jag var hemma.
He knew that I was home.

A colon is used before a direct quotation in place of the English comma:

Jag sade: »Jag talar svenska.»
I said, "I speak Swedish."

Exclamation marks are used more widely in Swedish than in English. They are used not only after imperatives and words of warning (e.g., *Skynda er!* Hurry up!), but also after words of address in a letter (e.g., *Käre vän!* Dear friend).

In the genitive case, no apostrophe is used before the -s ending (as in English "the boy's dog"), but it is used in place of the -s ending for the genitive of words ending in -s or -z (e.g., *Nils' rum*, Nils's room).

WORD ORDER

Normal and Inverted Word Order

Swedish and English share the same two kinds of word order: normal and inverted. In sentences in normal word order, the subject precedes the verb. In sentences in inverted word order, the subject comes after the verb:

Han är min vän. (NORMAL)
He is my friend.

Vem har min bil? (NORMAL)
Who has my car?

Är ni hemma? (INVERTED)
Are you home?

Inverted word order is rare in English except in questions, and, as the second example above indicates, even in questions it is not mandatory. In Swedish, however, inverted word order is very frequent, and is often used in instances where the English equivalent would have normal word order. Inverted word order is used in independent clauses in the following constructions in Swedish:

1. In interrogative sentences in which the subject is not an interrogative pronoun:

Talar ni svenska?
Do you speak Swedish?

2. When the independent clause is preceded by a dependent clause:

Sedan de hade gått, gick jag hem.
After they had gone, I went home.

3. When the independent clause begins with an adverb or an adverbial phrase:

Nu är jag hemma.
Now I am home.

Nästa sommar skall jag resa till Sverige.
Next summer I shall go to Sweden.

4. When the object of the independent clause precedes the subject:

Den här boken har jag köpt i Stockholm.
This book I bought in Stockholm.

For the most part, dependent clauses have normal word order:

Han vet, att jag inte är hemma.
He knows that I am not home.

Position of Adverbs

In clauses with normal word order, adverbs usually come immediately after the verb (after the auxiliary verb in compound tenses):

Vi var nu hemma.
We were now home.

Han hade redan gått hem.
He had already gone home.

A few adverbs, however, precede the verb (the auxiliary verb in compound tenses) in dependent clauses:

Han visste, att jag redan hade gått.
He knew that I had already left.

The most important adverbs of this kind are:

aldrig (never)	garna (gladly)
alltid (always)	icke (not)
antagligen (probably)	inte (not)
ej (not)	kanske (perhaps)

möjligen (possibly)   snart (soon)
ofta (often)   sällan (seldom)
redan (already)

In independent clauses in normal word order, however, even these adverbs come after the verb. In independent clauses in inverted word order, they are placed immediately after the subject:

Är han inte hemma?
Is he not home?

Position of Indirect Objects

Indirect objects, when used without a preposition, are placed before the direct object:

Jag gav honom det.
[I gave him it.]
I gave it to him.

HOW TO FORM QUESTIONS

In Swedish, statements in both normal and inverted word order can be changed into questions simply by retaining the original word order and raising the tone of the voice at the end of the sentence:

Nu är du hemma.	Now you are home.
Nu är du hemma?	Are you home now?

For statements in normal word order, a question can be formed by inverting the word order:

Han lagade min bil.	He repaired my car.
Lagade han min bil?	Did he repair my car?

Interrogative Words

Many questions, in Swedish as in English, begin with an interrogative word, which may be an adverb, adjective or pronoun. "Why," "who" and "which" are examples of such words in English. In a Swedish question formed in this way, the verb generally follows immediately after the interrogative word. The most common question words in Swedish are the following:

ADVERBS

Var?	Where?	Var är kaféet? Where is the cafe?
Vart?	Where to?	Vart har han rest? Where has he gone to?
När?	When?	När gick ni? When did you leave?
Hur?	How?	Hur långt går ni? How far are you going?

15

Varför?	Why?	Varför går ni? Why are you going?

PRONOUNS

Vem?	Who? Whom?	Vem är det där barnet? Who is that child?
Vems?	Whose?	Vems glas är det där? Whose glass is that?
Vad?	What?	Vad skall jag göra? What shall I do?
Vilken? (Vilket, Vilka)	Who? What? Which?	Vilka är de där männen? Who are those men?

ADJECTIVES

Vilken? (Vilket, Vilka)	What? Which?	Vilket är mitt glas? Which glass is mine?

Vilken (vilket, vilka) is used both as a pronoun and as an adjective. *Vilka,* the plural form of *vilken,* is used in place of the missing plural of *vem.* When used pronominally, the genitive of *vilken (vilket, vilka)* is formed simply by adding the ending *-s:*

Vilkens glas är det där?
Whose glass is that?

When an interrogative pronoun serves as the subject of a question in a dependent clause, it is always followed by the relative pronoun *som:*

Vet ni, vem som har telefonerat?
Do you know who has telephoned?

NEGATION

Any Swedish sentence can be changed into its negative equivalent simply by using the word *inte* (no, not) in one of the following positions:

1. After the verb of an independent clause in normal word order:

Han lagade inte min bil.
He did not repair my car.

2. Before the verb of a dependent clause:

Jag vet, att han inte lagade min bil.
I know that he did not repair my car.

3. After the subject of an independent clause in inverted word order:

Är du inte min vän?
Are you not my friend?

The word for "no" is *nej*. The words for "yes" are *ja*, in response to a question expressed affirmatively, and *jo*, in response to a question expressed negatively, or in contradicting a negative statement.

NOUNS AND ARTICLES

Gender and the Indefinite Article

All nouns in Swedish are either common or neuter in gender. The indefinite article (English "a" or "an") has two forms, corresponding to these two noun genders. The common form of the indefinite article is *en;* the neuter form is *ett.* The best way to remember the gender of a noun is to memorize the appropriate indefinite article with it. Furthermore, although there are no hard and fast rules by which to determine noun gender according to meaning or form, there are some helpful correspondences between them.

Common Nouns

About three-quarters of all Swedish nouns are common in gender. To this category belong:

1. Most nouns denoting living things:

en man (a man)	en hund (a dog)
en kvinna (a woman)	en fisk (a fish)
en pojke (a boy)	en ek (an oak)

2. Nouns denoting seasons and festivals:

vår (spring)	vinter (winter)
sommar (summer)	jul (Christmas)
höst (autumn)	påsk (Easter)

3. Nouns ending in *-ad, -are, -dom, -het, -ing, -ion* or *-lek:*

en månad (a month)	en inbjudning (an invitation)
en läkare (a doctor)	en diskussion (a discussion)
en sjukdom (an illness)	en storlek (a size)
en nyhet (a novelty)	

Notice, however, that some nouns that might be expected to be common in gender, since they refer to living things, are in fact neuter (e.g., *ett barn*, a child, *ett bi*, a bee, *ett lejon*, a lion, *ett träd*, a tree).

Neuter Nouns

Neuter nouns include:

1. The names of most inanimate things:

ett hus (a house)	ett tak (a roof)
ett tecken (a sign)	ett segl (a sail)
ett fönster (a window)	ett bibliotek (a library)

2. Nouns ending in *-em, -iv, -eum* or *-ium:*

ett problem (a problem)	ett museum (a museum)
ett motiv (a motive)	ett laboratorium (a laboratory)

3. The names of countries, mountains, towns and the letters of the alphabet:

Sverige (Sweden)	Drottningholm
Stockholm	Europa (Europe)

Noun Declensions

There are five noun declensions (ways to form the indefinite plural of nouns) in Swedish.

First Declension

Approximately 10% of all Swedish nouns belong to the first declension. They are all common nouns, and the majority end in *-a* in the singular, which is dropped before the plural ending *-or:*

SINGULAR	PLURAL
en blomma (a flower)	blommor (flowers)
en hylla (a shelf)	hyllor (shelves)
en flicka (a girl)	flickor (girls)

A few first declension nouns end in a consonant:

SINGULAR	PLURAL
en ros (a rose)	rosor (roses)
en våg (a wave)	vågor (waves)
en svan (a swan)	svanor (swans)

Second Declension

Second declension nouns account for almost 40% of all Swedish nouns. With the exception of *finger* (finger), they are all common in gender. All take the plural ending *-ar*. The second declension includes:

1. Most monosyllabic common nouns ending in a consonant:

SINGULAR	PLURAL
en arm (an arm)	armar (arms)
en hund (a dog)	hundar (dogs)
en häst (a horse)	hästar (horses)

2. Some monosyllabic common nouns ending in a vowel:

SINGULAR	PLURAL
en fru (a wife)	fruar (wives)
en ö (an island)	öar (islands)
en sjö (a lake)	sjöar (lakes)

3. Most common nouns of more than one syllable ending in unstressed *-e*, *-el*, *-en* or *-er*. Note that these nouns drop the *-e-* when the plural ending is added:

SINGULAR	PLURAL
en gosse (a boy)	gossar (boys)
en fågel (a bird)	fåglar (birds)
en socken (a parish)	socknar (parishes)
en syster (a sister)	systrar (sisters)

4. Common nouns ending in -*dom* or -*ing:*

SINGULAR	PLURAL
en sjukdom (an illness)	sjukdomar (illnesses)
en drottning (a queen)	drottningar (queens)

5. There are a few second declension nouns that have irregular plural forms. These include:

SINGULAR	PLURAL
en afton (an evening)	aftnar (evenings)
en morgon (a morning)	morgnar (mornings)
en sommar (a summer)	somrar (summers)
en dotter (a daughter)	döttrar (daughters)
en moder (a mother)	mödrar (mothers)

Third Declension

Both common and neuter nouns are found in the third declension, which comprises about 20% of all Swedish nouns. The plural ending for this declension is -*er*. The main categories for third declension nouns are:

1. Many monosyllabic nouns ending in a consonant:

SINGULAR	PLURAL
en dam (a lady)	damer (ladies)
en park (a park)	parker (parks)

2. All nouns ending in -*eum* or -*ium*. In the plural these nouns drop the -*um* when the plural ending is added:

SINGULAR	PLURAL
ett museum (a museum)	museer (museums)
ett studium (a study)	studier (studies)

3. Some common nouns ending in a vowel. The plural ending for these nouns is -*r* instead of -*er:*

SINGULAR	PLURAL
en hustru (a wife)	hustrur (wives)
en jungfru (a maiden)	jungfrur (maidens)
en ko (a cow)	kor (cows)
en sko (a shoe)	skor (shoes)
en tå (a toe)	tår (toes)
en fiende (an enemy)	fiender (enemies)

4. Seventeen nouns, of which the most common are presented here, that modify their stem vowels in the plural:

SINGULAR	PLURAL
en brand (a fire)	bränder (fires)
en hand (a hand)	händer (hands)
ett land (a country)	länder (countries)
en strand (a beach)	stränder (beaches)
en tand (a tooth)	tänder (teeth)
en bokstav (a letter of the alphabet)	bokstäver (letters of the alphabet)
en son (a son)	söner (sons)
en stad (a town)	städer (towns)
en natt (a night)	nätter (nights)
en bok (a book)	böcker (books)
en fot (a foot)	fötter (feet)

Fourth Declension

Fourth declension nouns are very few in number, accounting for only about 5% of all Swedish nouns. They are all neuter nouns ending in a vowel in the singular. The plural ending for the fourth declension is -n:

SINGULAR	PLURAL
ett näste (a nest)	nästen (nests)
ett piano (a piano)	pianon (pianos)
ett bi (a bee)	bin (bees)

Two nouns in the fourth declension have irregular plural forms:

SINGULAR	PLURAL
ett öga (an eye)	ögon (eyes)
ett öra (an ear)	öron (ears)

Fifth Declension

Fifth declension nouns have no plural ending—the singular and plural forms are mostly identical. About 25% of all Swedish nouns fall within this declension. These include:

1. Most neuter nouns ending in a consonant.

SINGULAR	PLURAL
ett bad (a bath)	bad (baths)
ett barn (a child)	barn (children)
ett djur (an animal)	djur (animals)

2. Common nouns ending in -are or -ande, and some nouns ending in -er:

SINGULAR	PLURAL
en läkare (a doctor)	läkare (doctors)
en främmande (a stranger)	främmande (strangers)
en musiker (a musician)	musiker (musicians)

3. The following fifth declension common nouns are among those that show a vowel change in the plural:

SINGULAR	PLURAL
en gås (a goose)	gäss (geese)
en mus (a mouse)	möss (mice)
en fader (a father)	fäder (fathers)
en broder (a brother)	bröder (brothers)
en man (a man)	män (men)

The Definite Article

The Definite Article Singular

All the nouns presented thus far have been in the indefinite form, taking the indefinite articles *en* or *ett* in the singular. The Swedish definite article singular (equivalent to English "the") is very similar in form to the indefinite article and, like the indefinite article, it must agree in gender with the noun it modifies. It is always, however, added to the indefinite singular form of the noun as a **suffix.** In the singular, the definite article suffix for common nouns is *-en;* for neuter nouns it is *-et.* If the noun ends in a vowel, however, the two suffixes are shortened to *-n* and *-t:*

SINGULAR

INDEFINITE	DEFINITE
en son (a son)	sonen (the son)
en kvinna (a woman)	kvinnan (the woman)
ett barn (a child)	barnet (the child)
ett äpple (an apple)	äpplet (the apple)

A number of slight variations on the basic rules for the formation of the definite article suffix in the singular should be noted:

1. Both common and neuter nouns ending in unstressed *-en* drop the *-e-* when the definite article suffix is added:

SINGULAR

INDEFINITE	DEFINITE
en sägen (a legend)	sägnen (the legend)
ett vapen (a weapon)	vapnet (the weapon)

2. Neuter nouns ending in *-eum* or *-ium* drop the *-um* when the definite article suffix is added:

SINGULAR

INDEFINITE	DEFINITE
ett museum (a museum)	museet (the museum)
ett laboratorium (a laboratory)	laboratoriet (the laboratory)

3. Nouns ending in *-or* drop the *-e-* of the definite article suffix:

SINGULAR

INDEFINITE	DEFINITE
en doktor (a doctor)	doktorn (the doctor)
en professor (a professor)	professorn (the professor)

4. Common nouns ending in unstressed *-el* or *-er*, and some common nouns ending in weakly stressed *-el* or *-er*, drop the *e* of the definite article suffix:

SINGULAR

INDEFINITE	DEFINITE
en fågel (a bird)	fågeln (the bird)
en spegel (a mirror)	spegeln (the mirror)
en fjäder (a feather)	fjädern (the feather)
en moder (a mother)	modern (the mother)

5. Neuter nouns ending in unstressed *-el* or *-er* drop the *-e-* when the definite article suffix is added:

SINGULAR

INDEFINITE	DEFINITE
ett exempel (an example)	exemplet (the example)
ett finger (a finger)	fingret (the finger)

The Definite Article Plural

Unlike English, Swedish has not only two forms of the definite article in the singular, but also special forms in the plural. These forms are added as suffixes to the indefinite plural form of the noun:

1. For all common nouns, the definite article plural suffix is *-na:*

PLURAL

INDEFINITE	DEFINITE
blommor (flowers)	blommorna (the flowers)
armar (arms)	armarna (the arms)

2. Fourth declension nouns, which are all neuter, take the definite article plural suffix *-a* (the *-n-* of the *-na* suffix is dropped):

PLURAL

INDEFINITE	DEFINITE
äpplen (apples)	äpplena (the apples)
bin (bees)	bina (the bees)

3. Fifth declension neuter nouns take the definite article plural suffix *-en:*

PLURAL

INDEFINITE	DEFINITE
barn (children)	barnen (the children)
djur (animals)	djuren (the animals)

In the plural, as is the case in the singular, there are a few variations on the rules for the formation of the definite article suffix:

1. Neuter nouns ending in unstressed *-el*, *-en* or *-er* drop the *-e-* when the definite article plural suffix is added:

PLURAL

INDEFINITE	DEFINITE
exempel (examples)	exemplen (the examples)
vatten (waters)	vattnen (the waters)
fönster (windows)	fönstren (the windows)

2. There are a few important irregular definite article plurals:

PLURAL

INDEFINITE	DEFINITE
män (men)	männen (the men)
gäss (geese)	gässen (the geese)
ögon (eyes)	ögonen (the eyes)
öron (ears)	öronen (the ears)

Use of the Definite Article

The Swedish definite article is used for the most part as is its English equivalent. There are, however, some important exceptions to this rule. The names of days, seasons, festivals, streets and other public places usually take the definite article suffix. Nouns preceded by *båda* (both), *vardera* (either) or *ingendera* (neither) also take the definite article suffix.

The Genitive Case

In Swedish (as in English), nouns have two case forms: the nominative and the genitive. Nouns that function as the subject, the object or the indirect object of a clause in Swedish fall within the nominative case for which there are no special endings. To form the genitive, which expresses possession (e.g., the man's house), the ending -*s* is added to the nominative form of the noun. This ending, which is known as the *s*-genitive, is the same for both common and neuter nouns, singular and plural, in the indefinite and the definite declensions:

en mans hus	a man's house
mannens hus	the man's house
mäns arbete	men's work
männens arbete	the men's work
ett barns glas	a child's glass
barnets glas	the child's glass
barns glas	children's glasses
barnens glas	the children's glasses

NOTE: A noun preceded by a noun in the *s*-genitive does not take any definite article suffix.

The *s*-genitive is also used in a few common idiomatic expressions with the prepositions *i* and *till:*

i söndags	last Sunday
till bords	at table
till sängs	to bed

NOUNS AND ARTICLES

Table of Noun Forms

The following table presents the singular and plural forms, in the indefinite and definite declensions, for all five noun declensions.

SINGULAR

	INDEFINITE	DEFINITE
1ST DECLENSION	en blomma	blomman
2ND DECLENSION	en arm	armen
3RD DECLENSION	en dam	damen
	ett land	landet
4TH DECLENSION	ett äpple	äpplet
5TH DECLENSION	en resande	resanden
	ett barn	barnet

PLURAL

	INDEFINITE	DEFINITE
1ST DECLENSION	blommor	blommorna
2ND DECLENSION	armar	armarna
3RD DECLENSION	damer	damerna
	länder	länderna
4TH DECLENSION	äpplen	äpplena
5TH DECLENSION	resande	resandena
	barn	barnen

ADJECTIVES

Agreement of Adjectives with Nouns

The formation of adjectives in Swedish is quite simple and regular. Unlike its English equivalent, however, a Swedish adjective must agree in declension, gender and number with the noun it modifies. There are two declensions of adjectives in Swedish: (1) the indefinite declension, used for the most part when the modified noun is in the indefinite form;* (2) the definite declension, used when the modified noun takes the definite article suffix.

The Indefinite Declension

There are three adjectival endings for the indefinite declension, and these depend upon the gender and number of the qualified noun:

1. For singular common nouns, the uninflected form of the adjective is used:

en kall vinter	a cold winter
en grön fågel	a green bird

2. For singular neuter nouns, -t is added to the uninflected form of the adjective:

ett kallt bad	a cold bath
ett grönt blad	a green leaf

3. For the plural of both common and neuter nouns, -a is added to the uninflected form of the adjective:

kalla vintrar	cold winters
grona blader	green leaves

---

*All adjectives that are separated by a verb from the word they modify (e.g., *mannen är stor*, the man is large) take the indefinite declension.

The Indefinite Neuter Form of Adjectives

There are a few important rules relating to the formation of the indefinite neuter form of adjectives:

1. Adjectives ending in -*d* preceded by a consonant drop the -*d* and add the normal -*t* ending in the neuter. Adjectives ending in -*d* preceded by a long vowel drop the -*d* and add -*tt:*

en hård vinter	a hard winter
ett hårt exempel	a hard example
en röd sko	a red shoe
ett rött äpple	a red apple

2. Adjectives ending in -*t* preceded by a consonant remain unchanged in the neuter. Monosyllabic adjectives ending in -*t* preceded by a long vowel form the neuter normally:

en trött kvinna	a tired woman
ett trött barn	a tired child
en vit klänning	a white dress
ett vitt hus	a white house

3. Adjectives ending in unstressed -*en* drop the -*n* before the normal -*t* ending in the neuter:

en förmögen man	a wealthy man
ett förmöget hus	a wealthy house

4. Adjectives ending in a stressed vowel add -*tt* in the neuter:

en ny soffa	a new sofa
ett nytt hus	a new house

5. Adjectives ending in -*nn* drop an *n* when the -*t* ending is added in the neuter:

en tunn pojke	a thin boy
ett tunt barn	a thin child

The Definite Declension

There is only one adjectival ending in the definite declension: -*a* is added to the uninflected form of the adjective for both common and neuter nouns, singular and plural. In addition to this adjectival ending, however, a special definite article form must precede the adjective, while the modified noun retains its definite article suffix. The special definite article forms are: *den* (com. sing.), *det* (neut. sing.) and *de* (pl.):

den stora mannen	the big man
det stora barnet	the big child
de stora männen	the big men
de stora barnen	the big children

The Plural and the Definite Forms of Adjectives

1. Adjectives ending in unstressed -*al*, -*el*, -*en* or -*er* drop the -*a*- or -*e*- when -*a* is added to form the indefinite plural and the definite forms:

en enkel regel	a simple rule
enkla regler	simple rules
den enkla reglen	the simple rule
de enkla reglerna	the simple rules

2. The adjective *liten* (small) is irregular:

INDEFINITE

en liten flicka	a small girl
ett litet barn	a small child
små flickor	small girls
små barn	small children

DEFINITE

den lilla flickan	the small girl
det lilla barnet	the small child
de små flickorna	the small girls
de små barnen	the small children

3. When an adjective refers to a male entity in the definite singular, it may end in the old masculine termination -*e* instead of the usual -*a*. This form is normal in greetings, for which the definite article is also dropped:

Käre (Kära) vän!   Dear friend

Indeclinable Adjectives

Adjectives that end in *-a* or *-e* are indeclinable, retaining the same form in both genders, singular and plural.

en bra bok	a good book
ett bra barn	a good child
bra böcker	good books
bra barn	good children

Some of the more important indeclinable adjectives are *stilla* (quiet), *gyllene* (golden), *udda* (odd, as in "odd number") and *äkta* (genuine).

Use of Adjectives

Use of the Indefinite Form of Adjectives

The indefinite form of adjectives is used not only predicatively and after the indefinite articles *en* and *ett,* but also in the following constructions:

1. After the indefinite adjectives *mången* (many a), *någon* (some, any), *ingen* (no, not any) and *varje* (each, every):

mången kall vinter	many a cold winter
någon grön fågel	some green bird
inga gröna blader	no green leaves
varje vitt hus	every white house

2. After *vilken* and *sådan* in exclamations:

Vilken stor man!	What a large man!
En sådan kall vinter!	What a cold winter!

Use of the Definite Form of Adjectives

The definite form of adjectives is used (without the definite article) in the following constructions:

1. After a possessive adjective:

min stora hund	my large dog
mitt nya hus	my new house

2. After a demonstrative adjective:

denna stora hund	this large dog
detta nya hus	this new house
dessa stora hundar	these large dogs

3. When the adjective qualifies a proper noun:

vänliga Maria	kind Maria
gamla Fredrik	old Frederick

4. In forms of direct address:

Käre vän!	Dear friend
Bästa Herr Nilsson!	Dear Mr. Nilsson

5. After a noun in the genitive case:

Nilssons stora hund	Nilsson's large dog
Fredriks nya hus	Frederick's new house

Comparison of Adjectives

The majority of Swedish adjectives form the comparative by adding the ending -are, and the superlative by adding the ending -ast, to the uninflected positive form of the adjective. Those adjectives that end in unstressed -el, -en or -er in the positive, drop the -e- before the comparative or superlative ending. If the positive ends in -a, this vowel is dropped before the ending:

POSITIVE	COMPARATIVE	SUPERLATIVE
kall (cold)	kallare	kallast
enkel (simple)	enklare	enklast
mogen (ripe)	mognare	mognast
vacker (pretty)	vackrare	vackrast
ringa (humble)	ringare	ringast

Adjectives ending in -ad, -e or -isk, and all participles used as adjectives form the comparative and superlative with *mera* (more) and *mest* (most). These adjectives do not have comparative or superlative endings:

POSITIVE	COMPARATIVE	SUPERLATIVE
långlivad (long-lived)	mera långlivad	mest långlivad
öde (desolate)	mera öde	mest öde
typisk (typical)	mera typisk	mest typisk

A few adjectives take the comparative and superlative endings *-re* and *-st* (instead of *-are* and *-ast*). Most of these adjectives modify their stem vowels in the comparative and superlative forms:

POSITIVE	COMPARATIVE	SUPERLATIVE
hög (high, tall)	högre	högst
grov (coarse)	grövre	grövst
stor (large)	större	störst
tung (heavy)	tyngre	tyngst
ung (young)	yngre	yngst
låg (low)	lägre	lägst
lång (long)	längre	längst
trång (narrow)	trängre	trängst
få (few)	färre	

The following adjectives have irregular comparative and superlative forms:

POSITIVE	COMPARATIVE	SUPERLATIVE
dålig (bad, poor)	sämre	sämst
ond (bad, evil)	värre	värst
gammal (old)	äldre	äldst
god/bra (good)	bättre	bäst
liten (small)	mindre	minst
många (many)	flera	de flesta
mycken (much)	mera	mest
nära (near)	närmare	närmast OR näst

Declension of the Comparative and Superlative

The comparative is indeclinable: it has only one form for both genders, in the singular and plural, definite and indefinite:

INDEFINITE	DEFINITE
en kallare vinter	den kallare vintern
ett kallare bad	det kallare badet
kallare vintrar	de kallare vintrarna

The superlative, however, has an indefinite and a definite declension. The form ending in -ast or -st is indeclinable in the indefinite declension. This declension can only be used predicatively:

Den här studenten är högst.	This student is tallest.
Det här barnet är högst.	This child is tallest.
De här barnen är högst.	These children are tallest.

The definite form of superlatives ending in -ast adds -e to the superlative ending for both genders, singular and plural:

den kallaste vintern	the coldest winter
det kallaste badet	the coldest bath
de kallaste vintrarna	the coldest winters

The definite form of superlatives ending in -st adds -a to the superlative ending for both genders, singular and plural:

den största mannen	the largest man
det största barnet	the largest child
de största männen	the largest men

Use of the Comparative

The Swedish equivalent of English "than" is än. To form a comparison between two items, än is placed immediately after the adjective in the comparative form:

Han är yngre än jag.
He is younger than I.

Stockholm är större än Lund.
Stockholm is larger than Lund.

Comparison of Equality

To express equality (English "as . . . as"), the words *lika* . . . *som* are placed either side of the adjective in the positive form:

Han är lika trött som jag.
He is as tired as I.

ADVERBS

Adverbs Derived from Adjectives

Many Swedish adverbs are derived from adjectives simply by adding the ending -t to the common form of the adjective. Adverbs formed in this way have the same form as the indefinite neuter of the adjective:

ADJECTIVE	ADVERB IN -t
kall (cold)	kallt (coldly)
enkel (simple)	enkelt (simply)

Other Adverbs

There are some important adverbs in Swedish that are not derived from adjectives:

aldrig (never)	nyss (just now)
alltid (always)	någonsin (ever, anytime)
då (then, at that moment)	när (when)
då och då (now and then)	ofta (often)
förr (before)	redan (already)
genast (at once)	sedan (then, afterward)
ibland (sometimes)	snart (soon)
igen (again)	strax (immediately)
länge (a long time)	sällan (seldom)
nu (now)	ännu (still, yet)

Some adverbs of place have two forms, one used with verbs indicating motion and the other with verbs indicating rest:

INDICATING REST	INDICATING MOTION
borta (away)	bort
där (there)	dit
framme (ahead, there)	fram
här (here)	hit
hemma (home)	hem
inne (in)	in
nere (down)	ner
uppe (up)	upp
ute (out)	ut
var (where)	vart

Comparison of Adverbs

Adverbs derived from adjectives form comparatives and superlatives in the same way as the adjectives on which they are based:

ADVERB	COMPARATIVE OF ADVERB	SUPERLATIVE OF ADVERB
kallt	kallare	kallast
enkelt	enklare	enklast
högt	högre	högst

A few adverbs that are not derived from adjectives also have comparative and superlative forms:

ADVERB	COMPARATIVE OF ADVERB	SUPERLATIVE OF ADVERB
väl (well)	bättre	bäst
gärna (gladly)	hellre	helst
illa (badly)	värre	värst
mycket (very)	mera	mest
nära (near)	närmare	närmast

PRONOUNS

Personal Pronouns

Swedish personal pronouns have different forms according to their use and position in a sentence. The object form of a personal pronoun is used for both direct and indirect objects (i.e., after prepositions):

	SUBJECT FORM	OBJECT FORM
1ST PERS. SING.	jag (I)	mig (me)
2ND PERS. SING.	du (you)	dig (you)
	ni (you)	er (you)
3RD PERS. SING.	han (he)	honom (him)
	hon (she)	henne (her)
	den [COM.] (it)	den (it)
	det [NEUT.] (it)	det (it)
1ST PERS. PL.	vi (we)	oss (us)
2ND PERS. PL.	ni (you)	er (you)
3RD PERS. PL.	de (they)	dem (them)

Use of Personal Pronouns

The second person singular *du* is used when addressing relatives, close friends or children. The second person plural *ni* is used in the singular when addressing strangers. For polite address, however, the person's full name or title is normally used:

Vad önskar fru Svensson?
What do you want, Mrs. Svensson?

The third person singular forms *den* and *det* refer to common and neuter nouns respectively. In impersonal constructions (English "It is" or "there are"), *det* is used:

Det regnar.
It is raining.

Det är många män här.
There are many men here.

Reflexive Pronouns

Reflexive pronouns refer back to the subject of the clause (English "myself," "yourself," "himself," etc.). In Swedish, the first and second person reflexive pronouns, singular and plural, are identical to the corresponding object forms of the personal pronoun *(mig, dig, er, oss)*. The third person reflexive pronoun, singular and plural, is *sig:*

Jag har skurit mig.	I have cut myself.
Du har skurit dig.	You have cut yourself.
Ni har skurit er. (SING.)	You have cut yourself.
Han/Hon har skurit sig.	He/She has cut himself/ herself.
Vi har skurit oss.	We have cut ourselves.
Ni har skurit er. (PL.)	You have cut yourselves.
De har skurit sig.	They have cut themselves.

Possessive Adjectives

Possessive adjectives, as the name suggests, express possession (English "my," "your," "his," etc.). In Swedish, the first and second person possessive adjectives, both singular and plural, are declined according to the gender and number of the noun modified. The third person possessive forms, singular and plural, are indeclinable:

	COMMON	NEUTER	PLURAL
1ST PERS. SING.	min (my)	mitt	mina
2ND PERS. SING.	din (your)	ditt	dina
	er (your)	ert	era
3RD PERS. SING.	hans (his)	hans	hans
	hennes (her)	hennes	hennes
	dess (its)	dess	dess

	COMMON	NEUTER	PLURAL
1ST PERS. PL.	vår (our)	vårt	våra
2ND PERS. PL.	er (your)	ert	era
3RD PERS. PL.	deras (their)	deras	deras

Possessive adjectives are used in the same way as other adjectives:

Min hustru är hemma.   My wife is home.
Mitt hus är stort.   My house is large.
Mina barnen är unga.   My children are young.

The Possessive Reflexive Adjective

The third person possessive reflexive adjective *sin* corresponds to the reflexive personal pronoun *sig*. *Sin* is used to refer back to the subject of the clause in which it occurs, never to the subject of a previous clause. The Swedish possessive reflexive adjective (English "his," "her," "its," "their") must agree in gender and number with the noun it modifies. Its forms are *sin* (com. sing.), *sitt* (neut. sing.) and *sina* (pl.):

Hon skriver ett brev till sin man.
She is writing a letter to her (own) husband.

Hon skriver ett brev till sitt barn.
She is writing a letter to her (own) child.

Hon skriver ett brev till sina föräldrar.
She is writing a letter to her (own) parents.

When there is no reference back to the subject of the clause, the genitive forms of the third person pronouns are used. These non-reflexive forms are *hans*, *hennes*, *dess* and *deras* (see the preceding section, "Possessive Adjectives"):

Hon skriver ett brev till hennes man.
She is writing a letter to her (another woman's) husband.

Relative Pronouns

The most common relative pronoun in Swedish is the indeclinable *som*, which may be translated in English as "who," "whom," "that" or "which." *Som* may serve as the subject (Sentence 1) or as the direct object (Sentence 2) of a dependent clause:

1. Han har en vän, som bor i Oslo.
   He has a friend who lives in Oslo.

2. Han är en man, som jag känner.
   He is a man whom I know.

Som is not used, however, in the genitive case or with a preceding preposition. In a genitive construction, *som* is replaced by *vars* (whose, of which):

Flickan, vars vän han var, sade adjö.
The girl, whose friend he was, said good-bye.

The relative pronoun *vilken* (who, that, which) is also used in place of *som* in genitive constructions and with a preceding preposition. *Vilken* is declined as follows: *vilken* (com. sing.), *vilket* (neut. sing.) and *vilka* (pl.). When the relative pronoun refers back to an entire clause, the neuter form, *vilket*, is used:

Staden, till vilken jag kom, är stor.
The town to which I came is large.

Huset var vackert belägen, vilket gjorde mig mycket glad.
The house was beautifully situated, which made me very happy.

The genitive of *vilken (vilket, vilka)* is formed simply by adding the ending -*s*.

The relative pronoun *vad* (what, that), which is indeclinable, is also sometimes used:

Vi gör vad vi kan.
We are doing what we can.

Vad is used after the word *allt* (everything):

Hörde du allt, vad jag sade?
Did you hear everything that I said?

Demonstrative Pronouns and Adjectives

In English, the words "this," "that," "these" and "those" may function either as demonstrative pronouns or demonstrative adjectives. Swedish demonstratives may likewise be used adjectivally or pronominally. These demonstratives, which must agree in gender and number with the noun they modify, are declined as follows:

COMMON	NEUTER	PLURAL
denna (this)	detta	dessa
den här (this)	det här	de här
den (that)	det	de
den där (that)	det där	de där

Denna (detta, dessa), when used adjectivally, is followed by the noun in the indefinite declension. The other demonstrative adjectives, however, are followed by the noun in the definite declension:

Denna flicka är vänlig.	This girl is friendly.
Den här flickan är vänlig.	This girl is friendly.
Den flickan är vänlig.	That girl is friendly.
Den där flickan är vänlig.	That girl is friendly.
Detta barn är vänligt.	This child is friendly.
Det här barnet är vänligt.	This child is friendly.
Det barnet är vänligt.	That child is friendly.
Det där barnet är vänligt.	That child is friendly.
Dessa män är vänliga.	These men are friendly.
De här männen är vänliga.	These men are friendly.
De männen är vänliga.	Those men are friendly.
De där männen är vänliga.	Those men are friendly.

Although the demonstrative forms denna (detta, dessa) and den (det, de) are grammatically correct, the forms using här and där are considered to be more appropriate in conversation.

Other Pronouns

There are some other important pronouns in Swedish, some of which are presented here:

1. Indefinite pronouns and adjectives:

COMMON	NEUTER	PLURAL
man (one)		
någon (some, somebody)	något (some, something)	några
ingen (no, nobody, none)	inget OR intet	inga
somlig (some)	somligt	somliga
all (all)	allt	alla
mången (many, many a)	månget	många
var (each, every)	vart	
varje (each, every)	varje	
endera (either)	ettdera	
någondera (some one, either)	någotdera	
ingendera (no one, neither)	intetdera	

The indefinite pronoun *man* (one) is used very frequently in Swedish, often when "you" or "people" would be used in the equivalent English construction:

Man kan se Stockholms universitet härifrån.
You can see the University of Stockholm from here.

2. Indefinite relative pronouns:

vem som helst som	whoever
vem än	whoever
var och en som	whoever
vilken (vilket, vilka) som helst som	whoever, whatever, whichever
vad som helst som	whatever
vad än	whatever

These pronouns are used in the same way as the other relative pronouns:

Vem som helst som ämnar resa till Sverige bör lära sig svenska.
Whoever intends to travel to Sweden ought to learn Swedish.

3. The pronoun *själv* is used in Swedish to emphasize the noun or pronoun to which it refers. Its meaning is equivalent to English "myself," "ourselves," etc., in such expressions as "I went there myself," "we made it ourselves." *Själv* must agree in gender and number with the noun or pronoun to which it refers; its forms are *själv* (com. sing.), *självt* (neut. sing.) and *själva* (pl.):

Hon gjorde det själv.
She did it herself.

De gjorde det själva.
They did it themselves.

PREPOSITIONS

Although Swedish prepositions are often very similar in form to English prepositions, their meanings and use can differ considerably. Some of the more important prepositions are presented here along with examples of their usage:

av	of, by	Jag har en ring av guld. I have a ring (made) of gold. Hon köper en roman av Strindberg. She is buying a novel by Strindberg.
efter	after	De gick efter en halvtimme. They went after half an hour.
framför	before, in front of	Jag stod framför dörren. I stood in front of the door.
från	from	Han kom från Göteborg. He came from Gothenburg.
för	for	Vi köpte det för tjugo kronor. We bought it for twenty kronor.
genom, igenom	through	Jag körde genom Malmö. I drove through Malmö.
hos	with, at	Jag bor hos min vän. I am living with my friend.
i	in, on	Vi bor i Amerika. We live in America.

med	with	Jag talade med honom i telefon. I spoke with him on the telephone.
på	on, in, at	De gick hem på onsdag. They went home on Wednesday. Vi stod på gatan. We were standing in the street. Vi bor på Hilton. We are staying at the Hilton.
till	to	Tåget går till Stockholm. The train is going to Stockholm.
under	under	Han stod under bron. He stood under the bridge.
vid	beside, at	De väntade vid huset. They waited beside the house.
åt	to	Säg åt honom, att jag är hemma. [Say to him that I am home.] Tell him that I am home.
över	over, above, across	Fågeln flög över träden. The bird flew over the trees. Vi gick över torget. We walked across the square.

CONJUNCTIONS

Swedish, like English, has two major kinds of conjunction: coordinating conjunctions and subordinating conjunctions.

Coordinating Conjunctions

Coordinating conjunctions (e.g., "and," "or" and "but" in English) usually link together two or more independent clauses. The principal conjunctions of this type in Swedish are presented here along with examples of their usage:

och	and	Jag gick hem och skrev ett brev. I went home and wrote a letter.

både . . .
   och
	both . . .
	   and
		Jag dricker både te och kaffe.
		I drink both tea and coffee.

eller	or	Vill ni ha mjölk eller vatten? Would you like milk or water?

antingen
  . . . eller
	either
	  . . . or
		Jag går antingen till Stockholm eller till Malmö nästa sommar.
		I shall be going either to Stockholm or to Malmö next summer.

varken
  . . . eller
	neither
	  . . . nor
		När han kom, var han varken trött eller kall.
		When he arrived, he was neither tired nor cold.

| men | but | Han hade gärna velat komma, men han var sjuk. He would have liked to come, but he was sick. |

Subordinating Conjunctions

Subordinating conjunctions introduce dependent clauses (e.g., "that," "because" and "if" in English). Some of the more important conjunctions of this type are presented here along with examples of their usage:

att	that	Jag sade, att jag kunda resa. I said that I could go.
då	as, since	Då vi var trötta, stannade vi hemma. Since we were tired, we stayed at home.
därför att	because	Hon lärde sig svenska, därför att hon måste uppsöka Sverige. She learned Swedish because she had to visit Sweden.
fast	although	Fast han hade förandrat sig mycket, kände genast jag igen honom. Although he had changed a great deal, I recognized him at once.
förrän, innan	before	Vi skulle gå hem, förrän det regnar. We should go home before it rains.

om	if	Jag skulle inte gå, om jag vore som du. I should not go if I were you.
medan	while	Medan vi stod där, såg vi en kvinna gå in i en affär. While we stood there, we saw a woman go into a shop.
sedan	after	Sedan jag hade talat med herr Andersson, gick han på biograf. After I had spoken to Mr. Andersson, he went to the movies.

VERBS

Comparison of English and Swedish Verbs

To English speakers, Swedish verbs appear remarkably simple in construction. In Swedish, there is generally only one verbal form for the active indicative of each tense, regardless of person or number (e.g., *jag har,* I have; *han har,* he has; *de har,* they have). Moreover, in Swedish, the simple present tense is equivalent to the English simple present and progressive present.

Principal Parts of the Verb

The Swedish verb has five principal parts: infinitive, present, past, supine and past participle:

INFINITIVE	PRESENT	PAST	SUPINE	PAST PART.
komma (come)	kommer	kom	kommit	kommen

The principal parts of the Swedish verb are used in the same way as their English equivalents except for the following important differences. In Swedish, the supine, not the past participle, is used with the auxiliary verb *ha* (have) in the formation of the compound tenses (e.g., *jag har kommit,* I have come; *jag hade kommit,* I had come). The Swedish past participle is used only as an adjective after the auxiliary verbs *vara* (be) and *bli* (become), and in the periphrastic construction of the passive voice (see pp. 60–61).

The Four Conjugations

There are four conjugations in Swedish and these are distinguished by the four supine endings: *-at, -t, -tt* and *-it.*

51

First Conjugation

The majority of Swedish verbs belong to the first conjugation, including all verbs of foreign derivation ending in *-era*. The present tense ending for regular first conjugation verbs is *-ar*, the supine ending is *-at*, the past ending is *-ade* and the past participle ending is *-ad*:

INFINITIVE	PRESENT	PAST	SUPINE	PAST PART.
tala (speak)	talar	talade	talat	talad
kalla (call)	kallar	kallade	kallat	kallad

There are some important irregular verbs in the first conjugation. None of these irregular first conjugation verbs has a past participle form:

INFINITIVE	PRESENT	PAST	SUPINE
heta (be called)	heter	hette	hetat
kunna (be able)	kan	kunde	kunnat
leva (live)	lever	levde	levat
veta (know)	vet	visste	vetat
vilja (be willing)	vill	ville	velat

Second Conjugation

The supine ending for all second conjugation verbs is *-t*. Second conjugation verbs that have roots ending in a voiced consonant (see p. 8) take the present tense ending *-er*, the past tense ending *-de* and the past participle ending *-d*:

INFINITIVE	PRESENT	PAST	SUPINE	PAST PART.
ställa (put)	ställer	ställde	ställt	ställd
sända (send)	sänder	sände	sänt	sänd*

Verbs with roots ending in *-r* that belong to this class do not take the present tense ending *-er*:

INFINITIVE	PRESENT	PAST	SUPINE	PAST PART.
höra (hear)	hör	hörde	hört	hörd
lära (teach, learn)	lär	lärde	lärt	lärd

*If the root ends in *-d*, no further *-d* is added.

Second conjugation verbs that have roots ending in a voiceless consonant (see p. 8) take the present tense ending -er, the past tense ending -te and the past participle ending -t:

INFINITIVE	PRESENT	PAST	SUPINE	PAST PART.
köpa (buy)	köper	köpte	köpt	köpt
läsa (read)	läser	läste	läst	läst

Some of the more important irregular verbs of the second conjugation are:

INFINITIVE	PRESENT	PAST	SUPINE	PAST PART.
böra (ought to)	bör	borde	bort	——*
göra (make)	gör	gjorde	gjort	gjord
lägga (lay)	lägger	lade	lagt	lagd
spörja (ask)	spörjer	sporde	sport	spord
säga (say)	säger	sade	sagt	sagd
välja (choose)	väljer	valde	valt	vald

Third Conjugation

Verbs of the third conjugation are very few in number. The infinitive of these verbs does not end in -a. The present tense ending is -r, the supine ending is -tt, the past participle ending is -dd and the past tense ending is -dde:

INFINITIVE	PRESENT	PAST	SUPINE	PAST PART.
gro (grow)	gror	grodde	grott	grodd
tro (believe)	tror	trodde	trott	trodd

Some of the more important irregular verbs of the third conjugation are:

INFINITIVE	PRESENT	PAST	SUPINE	PAST PART.
be (ask)	ber	bad	bett	bedd
dö (die)	dör	dog	dött	——

---

*Some Swedish verbs do not have past participle forms.

INFINITIVE	PRESENT	PAST	SUPINE	PAST PART.
få (get, be allowed)	får	fick	fått	/and/fådd*
gå (go)	går	gick	gått	gången
se (see)	ser	såg	sett	sedd
stå (stand)	står	stod	stått	/för/stådd

Fourth Conjugation

The supine ending for fourth conjugation verbs is -it, the present tense ending is -er or -r and the past participle ending is -en. The past tense, however, is not formed by adding an ending, but by an alteration of the stem vowel. Verbs that undergo vowel changes of this kind are known as strong verbs; they are subdivided into four classes according to the type of vowel change that takes place:

	INFINITIVE	PRESENT	PAST	SUPINE	PAST PART.
CLASS I	springa (run, burst)	springer	sprang	sprungit	sprungen
CLASS II	skriva (write)	skriver	skrev	skrevit	skriven
CLASS III	bjuda (offer)	bjuder	bjod	bjudit	bjuden
CLASS IV	bära (bear, carry)	bär	bar	burit	buren

Principal Parts of Common Strong Verbs

The following list contains the principal parts of the more common strong verbs in Swedish.

INFINITIVE	PRESENT	PAST	SUPINE	PAST PART.
binda (bind)	binder	band	bundit	bunden
bita (bite)	biter	bet	bitit	biten

---

*The most common compound form has been given in cases where the past participle is used for the most part only in compounds. Since the meaning of a compound form can differ considerably from that of the basic verb, a dictionary should be consulted.

INFINITIVE	PRESENT	PAST	SUPINE	PAST PART.
brinna (burn)	brinner	brann	brunnit	brunnen
brista (burst)	brister	brast	brustit	brusten
bryta (break)	bryter	bröt	brutit	bruten
bära (bear)	bär	bar	burit	buren
dra/ga/* (draw, pull)	dra/ge/r	drog	dragit	dragen
dricka (drink)	dricker	drack	druckit	drucken
driva (drive)	driver	drev	drivit	driven
falla (fall)	faller	föll	fallit	fallen
fara (go)	far	for	farit	/hädan/ faren**
finna (find)	finner	fann	funnit	funnen
flyga (fly)	flyger	flög	flugit	/bort/flugen
flyta (float)	flyter	flöt	flutit	fluten
frysa (freeze)	fryser	frös	frusit	frusen
försvinna (disappear)	försvinner	försvann	försvunnit	försvunnen
gala (crow)	gal	gol	galit	——
ge OR giva (give)	ger OR giver	gav	gett OR givit	given
gjuda (cast)	gjuter	göt	gjutit	gjuten
glida (glide)	glider	gled	glidit	——
gnida (rub)	gnider	gned	gnidit	gniden
gripa (seize)	griper	grep	gripit	gripen
gråta (weep)	gråter	grät	gråtit	/be/gråten
hinna (have time)	hinner	hann	hunnit	hunnen
hugga (cut)	hugger	högg	huggit	huggen
hålla (hold)	håller	höll	hållit	hållen
kliva (stride)	kliver	klev	klivit	/upp/kliven
klyva (cleave)	klyver	klöv	kluvit	kluven
knipa (pinch)	kniper	knep	knipit	knipen
knyta (tie)	knyter	knöt	knutit	knuten
komma (come)	kommer	kom	kommit	kommen
krypa (creep)	kryper	kröp	krupit	krupen

*The full forms of infinitives given in this list are used only in the written language and usually to indicate an elevated style.

**The most common compound form has been given in cases where the past participle is used for the most part only in compounds. A dictionary should be consulted for the meaning of these compounds.

56   VERBS

INFINITIVE	PRESENT	PAST	SUPINE	PAST PART.
lida (suffer)	lider	led	lidit	liden
ligga (lie down)	ligger	låg	legat	/för/legad
ljuda (sound)	ljuder	ljöd	ljudit	——
ljuga (tell a lie)	ljuger	ljög	ljugit	/be/ljugen
låta (allow, sound)	låter	lät	låtit	/över/låten
niga (curtsy)	niger	neg	nigit	——
njuta (enjoy)	njuter	njöt	njutit	njuten
pipa (pipe)	piper	pep	pipit	——
rida (ride)	rider	red	ridit	riden
rinna (run, flow)	rinner	rann	runnit	runnen
riva (tear)	river	rev	rivit	riven
ryta (roar)	ryter	röt	rutit	ruten
sitta (sit)	sitter	satt	suttit	/för/sutten
sjuda (seethe)	sjuder	sjöd	sjudit	sjuden
sjunga (sing)	sjunger	sjöng	sjungit	sjungen
sjunka (sink)	sjunker	sjönk	sjunkit	sjunken
skina (shine)	skiner	sken	skinit	——
skjuta (shoot)	skjuter	sköt	skjutit	skjuten
skrida (glide, proceed)	skrider	skred	skridit	/över/ skriden
skrika (scream)	skriker	skrek	skrikit	/ut/skriken
skriva (write)	skriver	skrev	skrivit	skriven
skryta (boast)	skryter	skröt	skrutit	/om/ skruten
skära (cut)	skär	skar	skurit	skuren
slippa (escape)	slipper	slapp	sluppit	/upp/ sluppen
slita (tear)	sliter	slet	slitit	sliten
sluta (close)	sluter	slöt	slutit	sluten
slå (strike)	slår	slog	slagit	slagen
smyga (slip)	smyger	smög	smugit	/in/smugen
snyta (blow the nose)	snyter	snöt	snutit	/o/snuten
sova (sleep)	sover	sov	sovit	——
spinna (spin)	spinner	spann	spunnit	spunnen
spricka (burst)	spricker	sprack	spruckit	sprucken
sprida (spread)	sprider	spred OR spridde	spritt	spridd
springa (run, burst)	springer	sprang	sprungit	sprungen

INFINITIVE	PRESENT	PAST	SUPINE	PAST PART.
spritta (start up)	spritter	spratt	———	———*
sticka (stick)	sticker	stack	stuckit	stucken
stiga (rise)	stiger	steg	stigit	stigen
stjäla (steal)	stjäl	stal	stulit	stulen
strida (fight)	strider	stred OR stridde	stridit OR stritt	/be/stridd
stryka (stroke)	stryker	strök	strukit	struken
supa (tipple)	super	söp	supit	/för/supen
svida (ache)	svider	sved	svidit	———
svika (deceive)	sviker	svek	svikit	sviken
svär/j/a (swear)	svär	svor	svurit	svuren
ta/ga/ (take)	ta/ge/r	tog	tagit	tagen
tiga (be silent)	tiger	teg	tegat	/för/tegen
tjuta (howl)	tjuter	tjöt	tjutit	———
vika (fold)	viker	vek	vikit	viken OR vikt
vina (whine)	viner	ven	vinit	———
vinna (win)	vinner	vann	vunnit	vunnen
vrida (twist)	vrider	vred	vridit	vriden
äta (eat)	äter	åt	ätit	äten

"To Be"

In Swedish, there are two ways in which to express the meaning of the English "to be." The verb *vara* is used to denote a fixed state of being (e.g., *det är kallt*, it is cold), whereas the verb *bli* denotes a transition from one state of being to another and is closer in meaning to the English "become" (e.g., *det börjar bli kallt*, it is getting cold). The principal parts of the verbs *vara* and *bli* are:

INFINITIVE	PRESENT	PAST	SUPINE	PAST PART.
vara	är	var	varit	———
bli	blir	blev	blivit	bliven

---

*The verb *spritta* (start up) has neither a supine nor a past participle form.

Auxiliary Verbs

The verb *ha* (have) is used in Swedish (as in English) as an auxiliary in the formation of compound tenses. The principal parts of *ha* are:

INFINITIVE	PRESENT	PAST	SUPINE	PAST PART.
ha	har	hade	haft	havd

Some of the other important auxiliary verbs are *skola* (be obliged), *vilja* (be willing), *kunna* (be able), *böra* (ought to) and *töra* (may). None of these verbs has a past participle form, and *töra* also lacks a supine form:

INFINITIVE	PRESENT	PAST	SUPINE
skola	skall	skulle	skolat
vilja	vill	ville	velat
kunna	kan	kunde	kunnat
böra	bör	borde	bort
töra	tör	torde	——

The Future Tense

There are three common ways in which the future tense can be formed in Swedish. In the case of verbs of motion and the verbs *vara* and *bli*, the present tense form is often used with a future meaning. The context will make the meaning clear in instances of this kind:

De kommer i morgon.
They will come tomorrow.

Är du tillbaka till klockan två?
Will you be back by two o'clock?

To express simple futurity without the sense of an intention, the phrase *kommer att* and the infinitive of the verb are used:

Jag kommer att resa i kväll.
I shall leave tonight.

If, however, there is the sense of an intention, the future tense is formed by using the present tense form of the auxiliary verb *skola* and the infinitive of the main verb:

Jag skall tala i kväll.
I shall speak tonight.

The Conditional

The conditional mood is used to express uncertainty or possibility (in English, characterized by the use of "would"). The present conditional is formed in Swedish by using the past form (*skulle*) of the verb *skola* and the infinitive of the main verb:

De skulle komma.
They would come.

Vi visste inte, vad som skulle hända.
We did not know what would happen.

The Perfect Tenses

The Present Perfect and Past Perfect

The present perfect and past perfect tenses are formed by using the present or past form of the auxiliary verb *ha* and the supine of the main verb:

Jag har talat.   I have spoken.
Vi har talat.   We have spoken.

Jag hade talat.   I had spoken.
Vi hade talat.   We had spoken.

The Future Perfect

The future perfect tense is formed by using the present tense form (*skall*) of the auxiliary verb *skola*, the infinitive *ha* and the supine of the main verb:

Jag skall ha talat.   I shall have spoken.
Vi skall ha talat.   We shall have spoken.

The Conditional Perfect

The conditional perfect tense is formed by using the past form (*skulle*) of the auxiliary verb *skola*, the infinitive *ha* and the supine of the main verb:

De skulle ha kommit.
They would have come.

Jag skulle ha skrivit.
I would have written.

The Imperative

The imperative (or command) form of first and third conjugation verbs is identical to the active infinitive (see p. 62). The imperative of second and fourth conjugation verbs is formed, however, simply by dropping the ending -*a* from the infinitive:

	INFINITIVE	IMPERATIVE
1ST CONJUGATION	tala	Tala mig! (Speak to me!)
2ND CONJUGATION	höra	Hör mig! (Listen to me!)
3RD CONJUGATION	tro	Tro mig! (Believe me!)
4TH CONJUGATION	finna	Finn mig! (Find me!)

The Passive Voice

Transitive verbs in Swedish may be active (as in the paradigms given so far) or passive. In a passive construction, the subject of the verb is acted upon (e.g., "I am asked"). In Swedish, the passive can be formed in one of two ways:

1. With the auxiliary verb *bli* and the past participle of the main verb. This construction is the most frequently used. Generally it refers to a single action or event rather than to a habitual or repeated action. The past participle is declined as an adjective in this construction and must agree in gender and number with the subject of the clause (see pp. 63–64 for the declension of the past participle):

> Bilen blev köpt av en ung man.
> The car was bought by a young man.

> Huset blev brunnet av den unga mannen.
> The house was burned by the young man.

2. By adding the ending *-s* to the active form of the verb. In the first conjugation, if the active form of the verb ends in *-r*, the *-r* is dropped when the *-s* ending is added. In the other conjugations, if the active form of the verb ends in *-er*, the *-e-* is usually dropped in the spoken language. The *-s* form of the passive is used to denote habitual or repeated action:

> Biblioteket öppnas klockan nio.
> The library opens at nine o'clock.

One of the most common uses of the *s*-passive is to express reciprocal action:

> Vi träffas på gatan i morgon.
> We shall meet each other on the street tomorrow.

Deponent Verbs

Deponent verbs are verbs that have a passive form but an active meaning. There are a number of deponent verbs in Swedish, and these have only passive forms with the *-s* ending:

> Han tycktes sova.
> He seemed to be asleep.

> De minns inte, vad jag sade.
> They don't remember what I said.

Other common deponent verbs include *andas* (breathe), *hoppas* (hope) and *lyckas* (manage).

The Infinitive

Swedish infinitives end in -*a* in the first, second and fourth conjugations. Third conjugation infinitives lack the -*a* ending. The passive of infinitives is formed simply by adding the ending -*s* to the active infinitive. Infinitives are usually preceded by *att* (equivalent to English "to"):

	ACTIVE	PASSIVE
1ST CONJUGATION	att tala (to speak)	att talas (to be spoken)
2ND CONJUGATION	att ställa (to put)	att ställas (to be put)
3RD CONJUGATION	att tro (to believe)	att tros (to be believed)
4TH CONJUGATION	att springa (to run, to burst)	att springas (to be run, to be burst)

There are, however, a few exceptions to the use of *att* before the infinitive. When an infinitive is used to express an intention, it is preceded by *för att* (in order to):

Vi gick till stationen för att hämta vårt bagage.
We went to the station to fetch our baggage.

The infinitive is also used without a preposition after auxiliary verbs and after a few other verbs that include *tänka* (contemplate), *hoppas* (hope), *tyckas* (seem), *bruka* (be in the habit of), *behöva* (need) and *önska* (wish).

Participles

Present Participles

In Swedish, present participles can be used either as adjectives or as nouns. Unlike their English equivalents, however, Swedish present participles are not used to form progressive tenses (e.g., English "I am walking"). In the first, second and fourth conjugations, present participles are formed by adding the ending -*ande* to the verb stem. In the third conjugation, they are formed by adding the ending -*ende* to the verb stem:

	INFINITIVE	PRESENT PARTICIPLE
1ST CONJUGATION	tala (speak)	talande (speaking)
2ND CONJUGATION	gömma (hide)	gömmande (hiding)
3RD CONJUGATION	fly (flee)	flyende (fleeing)
4TH CONJUGATION	springa (run, burst)	springande (running, bursting)

When used as adjectives, present participles are indeclinable:

Jag såg den flyende mannen.
I saw the fleeing man.

Jag såg de flyende männen.
I saw the fleeing men.

When used as nouns, present participles are declined according to the fifth declension:

De flyendena var oskyldiga.
Those fleeing were innocent.

Past Participles

Unlike their English equivalents, Swedish past participles are not used in the formation of the perfect tenses (e.g., English "I had spoken"). Swedish past participles are used as adjectives, after the auxiliary verbs *vara* and *bli* and as nouns. Past participles are declined like adjectives. The indefinite declension is as follows:

	COMMON	NEUTER	PLURAL
1ST CONJUGATION	talad (spoken)	talat	talade
2ND CONJUGATION	gömmd (hidden)	gömmt	gömmda
	köpt (bought)	köpt	köpta
3RD CONJUGATION	trodd (believed)	trott	trodda
4TH CONJUGATION	biten (bitten)	bitet	bitna

In the indefinite declension, past participles are used in the same way as adjectives in the indefinite:

Vi fann ett gömmt rum.
We found a hidden room.

Vi fann gömmda rum.
We found hidden rooms.

In the definite declension, the forms of past participles are identical to those of the indefinite plural. First conjugation participles, which end in -*ad*, add -*e* in the definite declension. All other participles add -*a* in this declension:

Vi fann det gömmda rumet.
We found the hidden room.

Vi fann de gömmda rumen.
We found the hidden rooms.

Compound Verbs

In the majority of cases, compound verbs in Swedish are formed by combining a simple verb form and a prefix. Such compound verbs fall into one of two categories depending on whether or not the prefix is detached from the verb in certain constructions: inseparable and separable compound verbs.

Inseparable Compound Verbs

Compound verbs formed with one of the following prefixes are inseparable:

*an*sluta (join)	*miss*bruka (misuse)
*be*tala (pay)	*sam*verka (cooperate)
*bi*träda (assist)	*um*gås (associate)
*er*sätta (replace)	*und*vika (avoid)
*för*klara (explain)	*van*vårda (neglect)
*här*leda (deduce)	åstunda (desire)

Compound verbs formed with a noun or adjective are also inseparable:

*full*ända (complete)	*råd*fråga (consult)
*god*känna (approve)	*tjuv*titta (peep at)

All these inseparable compound verbs are used in the same way as other verbs:

Författeren förklarade sin ny bok.
The author explained his new book.

Separable Compound Verbs

Compound verbs formed with an adverb or a preposition—
other than those listed in the preceding section, "Inseparable
Compound Verbs"—are generally separable:

*igen*känna (recognize)	*om*tycka (to like)
*med*följa (accompany)	*till*gå (happen)
*ned*lägga (put down)	*upp*söka (seek out)

The position of the separable prefix is determined in the following ways:

1. In the present and past participle forms of separable compound verbs, the prefix is not detached (e.g., *igenkännande, ned-
lagd*).

2. In compound tenses, the prefix is placed immediately after
the main verb:

Jag skall känna igen dig.
I shall recognize you.

Han har känt igen dig.
He has recognized you.

3. The adverbs *bra, mycket* and *illa* always come between the verb
and its separable prefix:

De tycker bra om henne.
They like her.

Jag tycker mycket om dig.
I think a great deal of you.

Jag tycker illa om dem.
I dislike them.

4. In independent clauses with normal word order, the verb and
its separable prefix are split by the following adverbs:

aldrig (never)	antagligen (probably)
alltid (always)	ej (not)

66   VERBS

gärna (gladly)   ofta (often)
icke (not)   redan (already)
inte (not)   snart (soon)
kanske (perhaps)   sällan (seldom)
möjligen (possibly)

5. In independent clauses with inverted word order, the subject of the clause comes between the verb and its separable prefix:

Tycker de om henne?
Do they like her?

Kände de igen honom?
Did they recognize him?

6. In dependent clauses, those adverbs that separate verb and prefix in independent clauses with normal word order precede the verb, which is followed immediately by its separable prefix:

Vi visste, att han alltid kände igen oss.
We knew that he always recognized us.

7. In all constructions other than those described above, the separable prefix is normally placed immediately after the verb.

Table of Verb Forms

The following table lists the verbal forms, active and passive, for all four conjugations, and includes the auxiliary verbs used in the formation of the compound tenses.

		1ST CONJUGATION	2ND CONJUGATION	3RD CONJUGATION	4TH CONJUGATION
INFINITIVE	ACTIVE	tala	ställa	tro	springa
	PASSIVE	talas	ställas	tros	springas
IMPERATIVE		tala	ställ	tro	spring
PRESENT	ACTIVE	talar	ställer	tror	springer
	PASSIVE	talas	ställes	tros	springes
PAST	ACTIVE	talade	ställde	trodde	sprang
	PASSIVE	talades	ställdes	troddes	sprangs
FUTURE	ACTIVE	skall tala	skall ställa	skall tro	skall springa
	PASSIVE	skall talas	skall ställas	skall tros	skall springas
CONDITIONAL	ACTIVE	skulle tala	skulle ställa	skulle tro	skulle springa
	PASSIVE	skulle talas	skulle ställas	skulle tros	skulle springas
PRESENT PERF.	ACTIVE	har talat	har ställt	har trott	har sprungit
	PASSIVE	har talats	har ställts	har trotts	har sprungits
PAST PERF.	ACTIVE	hade talat	hade ställt	hade trott	hade sprungit
	PASSIVE	hade talats	hade ställts	hade trotts	hade sprungits
FUTURE PERF.	ACTIVE	skall ha talat	skall ha ställt	skall ha trott	skall ha sprungit
	PASSIVE	skall ha talats	skall ha ställts	skall ha trotts	skall ha sprungits
CONDIT. PERF.	ACTIVE	skulle ha talat	skulle ha ställt	skulle ha trott	skulle ha sprungit
	PASSIVE	skulle ha talats	skulle ha ställts	skulle ha trotts	skulle ha sprungits

TELLING TIME

There are two ways in which to ask the time in Swedish: *Hur mycket är klockan?* or *Vad är klockan?* (What time is it?). The answer, too, may be expressed in one of two ways:

Klockan är två.   It is two o'clock.
Klockan är tolv.   It is twelve o'clock.

OR

Hon är två.   It is two (o'clock).
Hon är tolv.   It is twelve (o'clock).

Half hours are *halv tre* (half-past two), *halv ett* (half-past twelve). Fractional hours after the hour are expressed with *över,* and those before the hour with *i:*

en kvart över två   a quarter past two
en kvart i två   a quarter to two
fem över tolv   five past twelve
fem i tolv   five to twelve

USEFUL EXPRESSIONS

Listed below are some useful expressions that have not appeared in the main body of this grammar:

Var så god.	Please.
Tack.	Thanks.
God dag.	Hello.
God morgon.	Good morning.
God eftermiddag.	Good afternoon.
God kväll.	Good evening.
God natt.	Good night.
Gratulerar!	Congratulations!
Förlåt.	Excuse me.
Se upp!	Look out!
Bra.	All right.
Hur står det till?	How are you?
Tack bra, och ni själv?	Fine, thanks, and you?
Vad heter ni?	What is your name?
Jag heter	My name is . . . .
Talar ni engelska?	Do you speak English?
Jag talar inte mycket svenska.	I don't speak much Swedish.
Kan ni tala lite långsammare, tack?	Could you speak a little slower, please?
Vad heter det på svenska?	How do you say that in Swedish?
Vad önskar ni?	What would you like?
Vem är det?	Who is that?
Jag förstår.	I understand.
Jag förstår inte.	I don't understand.
Skulle ni kunna hjälpa mig?	Could you help me?
Hur långt är det till . . .?	How far is it to . . .?

69

A GLOSSARY OF GRAMMATICAL TERMS

E. F. BLEILER

This section is intended to refresh your memory of grammatical terms or to clear up difficulties you may have had in understanding them. Before you work through the grammar, you should have a reasonably clear idea what the parts of speech and parts of a sentence are. This is not for reasons of pedantry, but simply because it is easier to talk about grammar if we agree upon terms. Grammatical terminology is as necessary to the study of grammar as the names of automobile parts are to garagemen.

This list is not exhaustive, and the definitions do not pretend to be complete, or to settle points of interpretation that grammarians have been disputing for the past several hundred years. It is a working analysis rather than a scholarly investigation. The definitions given, however, represent most typical American usage, and should serve for basic use.

The Parts of Speech

English words can be divided into eight important groups: nouns, adjectives, articles, verbs, adverbs, pronouns, prepositions and conjunctions. The boundaries between one group of words and another are sometimes vague and ill-felt in English, but a good dictionary, like the Webster Collegiate, can help you make decisions in questionable cases. Always bear in mind, however, that the way a word is used in a sentence may be just as important as the nature of the word itself in deciding what part of speech the word is.

Nouns. *Nouns* are the *words* for *things* of all *sorts,* whether these *things* are real *objects* that you can see, or *ideas,* or *places,* or *quali-*

70

ties, or *groups* or more abstract *things. Examples* of *words* that are *nouns* are *cat, vase, door, shrub, wheat, university, mercy, intelligence, ocean, plumber, pleasure, society, army.* If you are in *doubt* whether a given *word* is a *noun,* try putting the *word* "my," or "this" or "large" (or some other *adjective*) in *front* of it. If it makes *sense* in the *sentence* the *chances* are that the *word* in *question* is a *noun.* [All the *words* in *italics* in this *paragraph* are *nouns.*]

Adjectives. Adjectives are the words that delimit or give you *specific* information about the *various* nouns in a sentence. They tell you size, color, weight, pleasantness and many *other* qualities. *Such* words as *big, expensive, terrible, insipid, hot, delightful, ruddy, informative* are all *clear* adjectives. If you are in *any* doubt whether a *certain* word is an adjective, add "-er" to it, or put the word "more" or "too" in front of it. If it makes *good* sense in the sentence, and does not end in "-ly," the chances are that it is an adjective. (Pronoun-adjectives will be described under pronouns.) [The adjectives in the *above* sentences are in italics.]

Articles. There are only two kinds of articles in English, and they are easy to remember. The definite article is "the" and the indefinite article is "a" or "an."

Verbs. Verbs *are* the words that *tell* what action, or condition or relationship *is going* on. Such words as *was, is, jumps, achieved, keeps, buys, sells, has finished, run, will have, may, should pay, indicates are* all verb forms. *Observe* that a verb *can be composed* of more than one word, as *will have* and *should pay,* above; these *are called* compound verbs. As a rough guide for verbs, *try adding* "-ed" to the word you *are wondering* about, or *taking* off an "-ed" that *is* already there. If it *makes* sense, the chances *are* that it *is* a verb. (This *does* not always *work,* since the so-called strong or irregular verbs *make* forms by *changing* their middle vowels, like *spring, sprang, sprung.*) [Verbs in this paragraph *are* in italics.]

Adverbs. An adverb is a word that supplies additional information about a verb, an adjective or another adverb. It *usually* indicates time, or manner, or place or degree. It tells you *how,* or *when,* or *where* or to what degree things are happening. Such words as *now, then, there, not, anywhere, never, somehow, always, very* and most words ending in "-ly" are *ordinarily* adverbs. [Italicized words are adverbs.]

Pronouns.   Pronouns are related to nouns, and take their place. (Some grammars and dictionaries group pronouns and nouns together as substantives.) *They* mention persons, or objects of any sort without actually giving their names.

There are several different kinds of pronouns. (1) Personal pronouns: by a grammatical convention *I, we, me, mine, us, ours* are called first person pronouns, since *they* refer to the speaker; *you* and *yours* are called second person pronouns, since *they* refer to the person addressed; and *he, him, his, she, her, hers, they, them, theirs* are called third person pronouns, since *they* refer to the things or persons discussed. (2) Demonstrative pronouns: *this, that, these, those.* (3) Interrogative, or question, pronouns: *who, whom, what, whose, which.* (4) Relative pronouns, or pronouns *that* refer back to something already mentioned: *who, whom, that, which.* (5) Others: *some, any, anyone, no one, other, whichever, none,* etc.

Pronouns are difficult for *us*, since our categories are not as clear as in some other languages, and *we* use the same words for *what* foreign-language speakers see as different situations. First, our interrogative and relative pronouns overlap, and must be separated in translation. The easiest way is to observe whether a question is involved in the sentence. Examples: "*Which* [int.] do *you* like?" "The hotel, *which* [rel.] was not far from the airport, had a restaurant." "*Who* [int.] is there?" "*I* don't know *who* [int.] was there." "The porter *who* [rel.] took our bags was Number 2132." *This* may seem to be a trivial difference to an English speaker, but in some languages *it* is very important.

Secondly, there is an overlap between pronouns and adjectives. In some cases the word "this," for example, is a pronoun; in other cases *it* is an adjective. *This* also holds true for *his, its, her, any, none, other, some, that, these, those* and many other words. Note whether the word in question stands alone or is associated with another word. Examples: "*This* [pronoun] is mine." "This [adj.] taxi has no springs." Watch out for the word "that," which can be a pronoun or an adjective or a conjunction. And remember that "my," "your," "our" and "their" are always adjectives. [All pronouns in this section are in italics.]

Prepositions.   Prepositions are the little words that introduce phrases that tell *about* condition, time, place, manner, association, degree and similar topics. Such words as *with, in, beside, under, of, to, about, for* and *upon* are prepositions. In English prepositions and adverbs overlap, but, as you will see *by* checking *in* your dictionary, there are usually differences *of* meaning *between* the two uses. [Prepositions *in* this paragraph are designated *by* italics.]

Conjunctions.   Conjunctions are joining-words. They enable you to link words *or* groups of words into larger units, *and* to build compound *or* complex sentences out of simple sentence units. Such words as *and, but, although, or, unless* are typical conjunctions. *Although* most conjunctions are easy enough to identify, the word "that" should be watched closely to see *that* it is not a pronoun *or* an adjective. [Conjunctions italicized.]

Words about Verbs

Verbs are responsible for most of the terminology in this short grammar. The basic terms are:

Conjugation.   In many languages verbs fall into natural groups, according to the way they make their forms. These groupings are called conjugations, and are an aid to learning grammatical structure. Though it may seem difficult at first to speak of First and Second Conjugations, these are simply short ways of saying that verbs belonging to these classes make their forms according to certain consistent rules, which you can memorize.

Infinitive.   This is the basic form that most dictionaries give for verbs in most languages, and in most languages it serves as the basis for classifying verbs. In English (with a very few exceptions) it has no special form. To find the infinitive for any English verb, just fill in this sentence: "I like to . . . . (walk, run, jump, swim, carry, disappear, etc.)." The infinitive in English is usually preceded by the word "to."

Tense.   This is simply a formal way of saying "time." In English we think of time as being broken into three great segments: past, present and future. Our verbs are assigned forms to indicate this division, and are further subdivided for shades of meaning. We subdivide the present time into the present (I walk) and present progressive (I am walking); the past into the simple past (I walked), progressive past (I was walking), perfect or present perfect (I have walked), past perfect or pluperfect (I had walked); and future into simple future (I shall walk) and future progressive (I shall be walking). These are the most common English tenses.

Present Participles, Progressive (Continuous) Tenses.   In English the present participle always ends in -*ing*. It can be used as a noun or an adjective in some situations, but its chief use is in *forming* the so-called progressive or continuous tenses. These are made by *putting* appropriate forms of the verb "to be" before a present participle. "To walk" [an infinitive], for example, has the present progressive: I am *walking*, you are *walking*, he is *walking*, etc.; past progressive, I was *walking*, you were *walking*, and so on. [Present participles are in italics.]

Past Participles, Perfect Tenses.   The past participle in English is not *formed* as regularly as is the present participle. Sometimes it is *constructed* by adding "-ed" or "-d" to the present tense, as *walked, jumped, looked, received;* but there are many verbs where it is *formed* less regularly: *seen, been, swum, chosen, brought.* To find it, simply fill out the sentence "I have . . . ." putting in the verb form that your ear tells you is right for the particular verb. If you speak grammatically, you will have the past participle.

Past participles are sometimes used as adjectives: "Don't cry over *spilt* milk." Their most important use, however, is to form the system of verb tenses that are *called* the perfect tenses: present perfect (or perfect), past perfect (or pluperfect), etc. In English the present perfect tense is *formed* with the present tense of "to have" and the past participle of a verb: I have *walked*, you have *run*, he has *begun*, etc. The past perfect is *formed*, similarly, with the past tense of "to have" and the past participle: I had *walked*, you had *run*, he had *begun*. Most of the languages you are likely to study have similar systems of perfect tenses, though they may not be *formed* in exactly the same way as in English. [Past participles are in italics.]

Auxiliary Verbs.   Auxiliary verbs are special words that are used to help other verbs make their forms. In English, for example, we use forms of the verb "to have" to make our perfect tenses: I *have* seen, you *had* come, he *has* been, etc. We also use *shall* or *will* to make our future tenses: I *shall* pay, you *will* see, etc. French, German, Greek and Italian also make use of auxiliary verbs, but although the general concept is present, the use of auxiliaries differs very much from one language to another, and you *must* learn the practice for each language. [Auxiliary verbs are in italics.]

Reflexive.   This term, which sounds more difficult than it really is, simply means that the verb flexes back upon the noun or pronoun that is its subject. In modern English the reflexive pronoun always has "-self" on its end, and we do not use the construction very frequently. In other languages, however, reflexive forms may be used more frequently, and in ways that do not seem very logical to an English speaker. Examples of English reflexive sentences: "He washes himself." "He seated himself at the table."

Passive.   In some languages, like Latin, there is a strong feeling that an action or thing that is taking place can be expressed in two different ways. One can say, A does-something-to B, which is "active"; or B is-having-something-done-to-him by A, which is "passive." We do not have a strong feeling for this classification of experience in English, but the following examples should indicate the difference between an active and a passive verb: Active: "John is building a house." Passive: "A house is being built by John." Active: "The steamer carried the cotton to England." Passive: "The cotton was carried by the steamer to England." Bear in mind that the formation of passive verbs and the situations where they can be used vary enormously from language to language. This is one situation where you usually cannot translate English word for word into another language and make sense.

Impersonal Verbs.   In English there are some verbs that do not have an ordinary subject, and do not refer to persons. They are always used with the pronoun "it," which does not refer to anything specifically, but simply serves to fill out the verb forms. Examples: "It is snowing." "It hailed last night." "It seems to me that you are wrong." "It has been raining." "It won't do."

Words about Nouns

Declensions. In some languages nouns fall into natural groups according to the way they make their forms. These groupings are called declensions, and making the various forms for any noun, pronoun or adjective is called declining it.

Declensions are simply an aid to learning grammatical structure. Although it may seem difficult to speak of First Declension, Second, Third and Fourth, these are simply short ways of saying that nouns belonging to these classes make their forms according to certain consistent rules, which you can memorize. In English we do not have to worry about declensions, since almost all nouns make their possessive and plural in the same way. In other languages, however, declensions may be much more complex.

Agreement. In some languages, where nouns or adjectives or articles are declined, or have gender endings, it is necessary that the adjective or article be in the same case or gender or number as the noun it goes with (modifies). This is called agreement.

This may be illustrated from Spanish, where articles and adjectives have to agree with nouns in gender and number:

| una casa blanca | one white house | dos casas blancas | two white houses |
| un libro blanco | one white book | dos libros blancos | two white books |

Here *una* is feminine singular and has the ending *-a* because it agrees with the feminine singular noun *casa; blanca* has the ending *-a* because it agrees with the feminine singular noun *casa.* *Blanco,* on the other hand, and *un* are masculine singular because *libro* is masculine singular.

Gender. Gender should not be confused with actual sex. In many languages nouns are arbitrarily assigned a gender (masculine or feminine, or masculine or feminine or neuter), and this need not correspond to sex. You simply have to learn the pattern of the language you are studying in order to become familiar with its use of gender.

Case. The idea of case is often very difficult for an English-speaker to grasp, since we do not use case very much. Perhaps

the best way to understand how case works is to step behind
words themselves, into the ideas that words express. If you look
at a sentence like "Mr. Brown is paying the waiter," you can see
that three basic ideas are involved: Mr. Brown, the waiter and
the act of payment. The problem that every language has is to
show how these ideas are to be related, or how words are to be
interlocked to form sentences.

Surprisingly enough, there are only three ways of putting
pointers on words to make your meaning clear, so that your lis-
tener knows who is doing what to whom. These ways are: (1)
word order; (2) additional words; (3) alteration of the word
(which for nouns, pronouns and adjectives is called case).

Word order, or the place of individual words in a sentence, is
very important in English. For us, "Mr. Brown is paying the
waiter" is entirely different in meaning from "The waiter is paying Mr. Brown." This may seem so obvious that it need not be
mentioned, but in some languages, like Latin, you can shift the
positions of the words and come out with the same meaning for
the sentence, apart from shifts of emphasis.

Adding other elements, to make meanings clear, is also com-
monly used in English. We have a whole range of words like "to,"
"from," "with," "in," "out," "of," and so on, that show relation-
ships. "Mr. Jones introduced Mr. Smith to the Captain" is unam-
biguous because of the word "to."

Case is not as important in English as it is in some languages,
but we do use case in a few limited forms. We add an -'s to nouns
to form a possessive; we add a similar -s to form the plural for
most nouns; and we add (in spelling, though there is no sound
change involved) an -' to indicate a possessive plural. In pronouns, sometimes we add endings, as in the words "who,"
"whose" and "whom." Sometimes we use different forms, as in
"I," "mine," "me"; "he," "his," "him"; "we," "ours" and "us."

When you use case, as you can see, you know much more about
individual words than if you do not have case. When you see the
word "whom" you automatically recognize that it cannot be the
subject of a sentence, but must be the object of a verb or a preposition. When you see the word "ship's," you know that it means
"belonging to a ship" or "originating from a ship."

If you assume that endings can be added to nouns or pronouns or adjectives to form cases, it is not too far a logical leap to see that certain forms or endings are always used in the same circumstances. A preposition, for example, may always be followed by a noun or pronoun with the same ending; a direct object may always have a certain ending; or possession may always be indicated by the same ending. If you classify and tabulate endings and their uses, you will arrive at individual cases.

Miscellaneous Terms

Comparative, Superlative.   These two terms are used with adjectives and adverbs. They indicate the degree of strength within the meaning of the word. "Faster," "better," "earlier," "newer," "more rapid," "more detailed," "more suitable" are examples of the comparative in adjectives, while "more rapidly," "more recently," "more suitably" are comparatives for adverbs. In most cases, as you have seen, the comparative uses "-er" or "more" for an adjective, and "more" for an adverb. Superlatives are those forms that end in "-est" or have "most" prefixed before them for adjectives, and "most" prefixed for adverbs: "most intelligent," "earliest," "most rapidly," "most suitably."

The Parts of the Sentence

Subject, Predicate.   In grammar *every complete sentence* contains two basic parts, the subject and the predicate. *The subject,* if *we* state the terms most simply, is the thing, person or activity talked about. *It* can be a noun, a pronoun, or something *that* serves as a noun. *A subject* would include, in a typical case, a noun, the articles or adjectives *that* are associated with it and perhaps phrases. Note that in complex sentences, *each part* may have its own subject. [*The subjects of the sentences and clauses above* have been italicized.]

The predicate *talks about the subject.* In a formal sentence the predicate *includes a verb, its adverbs, predicate adjectives, phrases and objects*—whatever *happens to be present.* A predicate adjective *is an adjective* that *happens to be in the predicate after a form of the verb "to be."* Example: "Apples *are red.*" [Predicates *are in italics.*]

In the following simple sentences subjects are in italics, predicates in italics and underlined. *"Green apples are bad for your digestion."* "When *I go to Sweden, I always stop in Uppsala.*" "The man with the handbag is traveling to Malmö."

Direct and Indirect Objects.   Some verbs (called transitive verbs) take direct and/or indirect objects in their predicates; other verbs (called intransitive verbs) do not take objects of any sort. In English, except for pronouns, objects do not have any special forms, but in languages such as Greek, which have case forms or more pronoun forms than English, objects can be troublesome.

The direct object is the person, thing, quality or matter that the verb directs *its action* upon. It can be a pronoun, or a noun, perhaps accompanied by an article and/or adjectives. The direct object always directly follows *its verb,* except when there is also an indirect object present, which comes between the verb and the object. Prepositions do not go before direct objects. Examples: "The cook threw *green onions* into the stew." "The border guards will want to see *your passport* tomorrow." "Give *it* to me." "Please give me *a glass of red wine.*" [We have placed *direct objects* in this paragraph in italics.]

The indirect object, as grammars will tell you, is the person or thing for or to whom the action is taking place. It can be a pronoun or a noun with or without article and adjectives. In most cases the words "to" or "for" can be inserted before it, if not already there. Examples: "Please tell *me* the time." "I wrote *her* a letter from Norrköping." "We sent *Mr. Persson* ten kronor." "We gave *the most energetic guide* a large tip." [Indirect objects in this paragraph are in italics.]

Clauses: Independent, Dependent, Relative.   Clauses are the largest components/*that go to make up sentences.*/ Each clause, in classical grammar, is a combination of subject and predicate./ *If a sentence has one subject and one predicate,*/it is a one-clause sentence./ *If it has two or more subjects and predicates,*/it is a sentence of two or more clauses./

There are two kinds of clauses: independent (principal) and dependent (subordinate) clauses./ An independent clause can stand alone;/it can form a logical, complete sentence./ A dependent clause is a clause/*that cannot stand alone;*/it must have another clause with it to complete it./

A sentence containing a single clause is called a simple sentence./ A sentence with two or more clauses may be either a complex or a compound sentence./ A compound sentence contains two or more independent clauses,/and/these independent clauses are joined together with "and," "or" or "but."/ A complex sentence is a sentence/*that contains both independent and dependent clauses.*/

A relative clause is a clause/*that begins with a relative pronoun: who, whom, that, which.*/ It is by definition a dependent clause,/*since it cannot stand by itself.*/

[Each clause in this section has been isolated by slashes./ Dependent clauses have been placed in italics;/independent clauses have not been marked./]

INDEX

A CATALOG OF SELECTED
DOVER BOOKS
IN ALL FIELDS OF INTEREST

A CATALOG OF SELECTED DOVER
BOOKS IN ALL FIELDS OF INTEREST

CONCERNING THE SPIRITUAL IN ART, Wassily Kandinsky. Pioneering work by father of abstract art. Thoughts on color theory, nature of art. Analysis of earlier masters. 12 illustrations. 80pp. of text. 5⅜ × 8½.   23411-8 Pa. $3.95

ANIMALS: 1,419 Copyright-Free Illustrations of Mammals, Birds, Fish, Insects, etc., Jim Harter (ed.). Clear wood engravings present, in extremely lifelike poses, over 1,000 species of animals. One of the most extensive pictorial sourcebooks of its kind. Captions. Index. 284pp. 9 × 12.   23766-4 Pa. $11.95

CELTIC ART: The Methods of Construction, George Bain. Simple geometric techniques for making Celtic interlacements, spirals, Kells-type initials, animals, humans, etc. Over 500 illustrations. 160pp. 9 × 12. (USO)   22923-8 Pa. $9.95

AN ATLAS OF ANATOMY FOR ARTISTS, Fritz Schider. Most thorough reference work on art anatomy in the world. Hundreds of illustrations, including selections from works by Vesalius, Leonardo, Goya, Ingres, Michelangelo, others. 593 illustrations. 192pp. 7⅞ × 10¼.   20241-0 Pa. $8.95

CELTIC HAND STROKE-BY-STROKE (Irish Half-Uncial from "The Book of Kells"): An Arthur Baker Calligraphy Manual, Arthur Baker. Complete guide to creating each letter of the alphabet in distinctive Celtic manner. Covers hand position, strokes, pens, inks, paper, more. Illustrated. 48pp. 8¼ × 11.
                24336-2 Pa. $3.95

EASY ORIGAMI, John Montroll. Charming collection of 32 projects (hat, cup, pelican, piano, swan, many more) specially designed for the novice origami hobbyist. Clearly illustrated easy-to-follow instructions insure that even beginning papercrafters will achieve successful results. 48pp. 8¼ × 11.   27298-2 Pa. $2.95

THE COMPLETE BOOK OF BIRDHOUSE CONSTRUCTION FOR WOOD-WORKERS, Scott D. Campbell. Detailed instructions, illustrations, tables. Also data on bird habitat and instinct patterns. Bibliography. 3 tables. 63 illustrations in 15 figures. 48pp. 5¼ × 8½.   24407-5 Pa. $1.95

BLOOMINGDALE'S ILLUSTRATED 1886 CATALOG: Fashions, Dry Goods and Housewares, Bloomingdale Brothers. Famed merchants' extremely rare catalog depicting about 1,700 products: clothing, housewares, firearms, dry goods, jewelry, more. Invaluable for dating, identifying vintage items. Also, copyright-free graphics for artists, designers. Co-published with Henry Ford Museum & Greenfield Village. 160pp. 8¼ × 11.   25780-0 Pa. $9.95

HISTORIC COSTUME IN PICTURES, Braun & Schneider. Over 1,450 costumed figures in clearly detailed engravings—from dawn of civilization to end of 19th century. Captions. Many folk costumes. 256pp. 8⅜ × 11¾.   23150-X Pa. $11.95

THE INFLUENCE OF SEA POWER UPON HISTORY, 1660–1783, A. T. Mahan. Influential classic of naval history and tactics still used as text in war colleges. First paperback edition. 4 maps. 24 battle plans. 640pp. 5⅜ × 8½.
25509-3 Pa. $12.95

THE STORY OF THE TITANIC AS TOLD BY ITS SURVIVORS, Jack Winocour (ed.). What it was really like. Panic, despair, shocking inefficiency, and a little heroism. More thrilling than any fictional account. 26 illustrations. 320pp. 5⅜ × 8½.
20610-6 Pa. $7.95

FAIRY AND FOLK TALES OF THE IRISH PEASANTRY, William Butler Yeats (ed.). Treasury of 64 tales from the twilight world of Celtic myth and legend: "The Soul Cages," "The Kildare Pooka," "King O'Toole and his Goose," many more. Introduction and Notes by W. B. Yeats. 352pp. 5⅜ × 8½.
26941-8 Pa. $8.95

BUDDHIST MAHAYANA TEXTS, E. B. Cowell and Others (eds.). Superb, accurate translations of basic documents in Mahayana Buddhism, highly important in history of religions. The Buddha-karita of Asvaghosha, Larger Sukhavativyuha, more. 448pp. 5⅜ × 8½.
25552-2 Pa. $9.95

ONE TWO THREE . . . INFINITY: Facts and Speculations of Science, George Gamow. Great physicist's fascinating, readable overview of contemporary science: number theory, relativity, fourth dimension, entropy, genes, atomic structure, much more. 128 illustrations. Index. 352pp. 5⅜ × 8½.
25664-2 Pa. $8.95

ENGINEERING IN HISTORY, Richard Shelton Kirby, et al. Broad, nontechnical survey of history's major technological advances: birth of Greek science, industrial revolution, electricity and applied science, 20th-century automation, much more. 181 illustrations. ". . . excellent . . ,"—Isis. Bibliography. vii + 530pp. 5⅜ × 8¼.
26412-2 Pa. $14.95

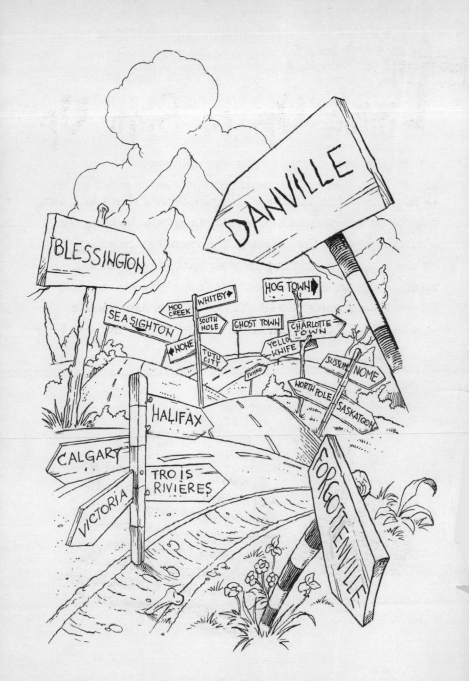

Mystery Cake

Christmas fruitcakes aren't as popular as they used to be. The younger crowd doesn't seem willing to give them the respect they deserve. They even make jokes about the same cakes being passed around like hot potatoes from one Christmas to the next. But folks in Manitou Springs, Saskatchewan, make sure that doesn't happen in their community. Each January they hold their Great Fruitcake Toss where they take up bats, golf clubs, slingshots, catapults or anything else that packs a wallop, and send their Christmas cakes sailing through the air.

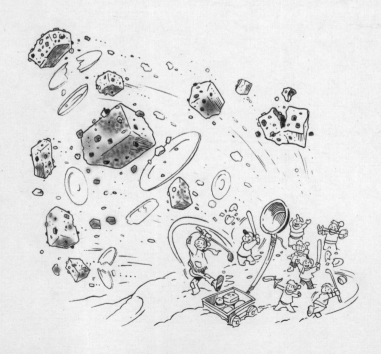